Tax Avoidance and European Law

Tax law is one of the legal fields with the most subtle influence on European integration and EU law. The European economic cooperation project emerged with the customs union, essentially a tax law concept, and evolved alongside other topics of tax harmonization. Still, the existence of the EU tax law is disputed. The research on the topic is significant, as the integration of national economies and markets has increased substantially, both within the EU and globally. This has put a strain on domestic tax rules, which are subject to the demands of the international taxation requirements.

This book explores the relationship between tax avoidance regulation and sovereignty within the European Union, analyzing the impact of the effective regulatory methods for limiting and eliminating aggressive tax planning by multinational companies. Focusing on analyzing good practice in fiscal regulation efficiency and the results generated by the tax jurisprudence both at national and European level, its main objective is to present the argument for inter-dependency between taxation and the current changes in the concept of sovereignty. It highlights where fiscal regulation has led to uniform, yet flexible, solutions for the actual fight against companies' abusive fiscal conduct, when taking advantage of tax competition.

This text will be of value to academics, researchers, and advanced students in tax law and tax avoidance regulation and their intersection with sovereignty in the context of the European Union.

Mihaela Tofan is Professor of Law at Alexandru Ioan Cuza University of Iasi, Romania, and Fulbright Senior Scholar Alumni at NYU School of Law, USA.

Routledge Research in Tax Law

Tax Avoidance and the Law
Selina Keesoony

Tax Avoidance and European Law
Redesigning Sovereignty Through Multilateral Regulation
Mihaela Tofan

Tax Avoidance and European Law

Redesigning Sovereignty Through Multilateral Regulation

Mihaela Tofan

Routledge
Taylor & Francis Group
LONDON AND NEW YORK

First published 2022
by Routledge
4 Park Square, Milton Park, Abingdon, Oxon OX14 4RN

and by Routledge
605 Third Avenue, New York, NY 10158

Routledge is an imprint of the Taylor & Francis Group, an informa business

British Library Cataloguing-in-Publication Data
A catalogue record for this book is available from the British Library

Library of Congress Cataloging-in-Publication Data
A catalog record for this book has been requested

ISBN: 978-1-032-31485-3 (hbk)
ISBN: 978-1-032-31486-0 (pbk)
ISBN: 978-1-003-30997-0 (ebk)

DOI: 10.4324/9781003309970

Typeset in Times New Roman
by Apex CoVantage, LLC

Contents

1 Introduction

All over the European Union (EU) and beyond, the everyday life routine for citizens has reached a general unprecedented level of globalization, described in patterns that largely rely on the continuous and significant efforts of public authorities. Mankind enjoys the personal comfort of individual featured living conditions, and equally has relatively high expectations to benefit from the social amenities and the collective facilities, derived from high quality public services, amenities and infrastructure. Only a small part of these functionalities is private, though their majority is provided by public services and the use of public goods, which indirectly, implies a large amount of money collected to the state budget. In other words, the citizens and residents' current everyday living is influenced in a decisive way by the quality of the public facilities offered by the public authorities, which is largely dependent on the amount of public spending. Sure enough, the state budget is a limited resource, so the public spending and the revenues must be balanced. Consequently, supplying a certain level of living for the citizens depends critically on the state budget's level of income, and that brings our analysis to tax regulatory policy, the most convenient tool to optimize public revenues.

Taxation is considered a field of precise knowledge and technicalities,[1] although everybody pays taxes, and the concept has been present in regulatory systems since the construction of the first form of public

1 The Quote Investigator ran an investigation on Albert Einstein's comment on filing tax returns, proving that the great mathematician said that filling the tax revenue form "is too difficult for a mathematician, it takes a philosopher" (https://quoteinvestigator.com/2011/04/15/einsotein-taxes-too-difficult/, retrieved on June 15, 2020). My opinion is that the required abilities are best fulfilled by a professional of law, mainly because of the dimension of effects of the tax specific regulation for all legal and natural persons, and secondly because the legitimacy of the taxation is governed by a complicated mixture of rules of law, soft law, and jurisprudential twists, both domestic and international.

DOI: 10.4324/9781003309970-1

authorities. Both legal field of expertise and public finance competencies are needed when using the conventional approach towards taxation and the "three Rs" (Revenue, Redistribution and Regulation) have to be addressed.[2]

Considering that in their desire for large budgets, governments manifest the tendency to tax everything,[3] their mission is more challenging in the context of global trade, because in cross-border transactions the competition for taxing all the revenue is tight. At least four scenarios are possible when looking for the right taxation principle:

1. taxation at source of the money jurisdiction
2. taxation at the residence jurisdiction of the parties
3. taxation at source jurisdiction of the income
4. taxation at the investor's residence jurisdiction, when borrowed capital is used

In such situations, possible double taxation situations may be addressed either by unilateral provisions, included in the domestic law of the interested countries, or by the application of the provisions included in double tax treaties. Still, neither unilateral provisions, nor double-tax treaties, are sufficient to prevent and, if needed, to eliminate the fiscal treatment colliding with the principle of tax neutrality.[4] There are particular situations when the valid connection that exists between the feature of a particular transaction and a precise state regulation (usually called nexus) requires the application of international law; for the European legal order, the legitimacy of the nexus should be analyzed directly, through the application of primary and secondary law, or indirectly, through the case-law of the Court of Justice of the European Union.[5]

Tax law is one of the legal fields with the most subtle influence on European integration and EU law. The European economic cooperation project

2 As Avi-Yonah has noted, the "three Rs" mesh surprisingly neatly with the three major taxes in most countries: the value-added tax (VAT) for revenue, the personal income tax (PIT) for redistribution, and the corporate income tax (CIT) for regulation. For details, see Reuven S. Avi-Yonah, The three goals of taxation, *Tax Law Review*, 60(1), 1–28, 2006.

3 Charles Kettering's quotation "Thinking is one thing no one has ever been able to tax" is referred by Henry Ejdelbaum, available at: www.aims.co.uk/%C2%93thinking-is-one-thing-no-one-has-ever-been-able-to-tax-%C2%94-charles-kettering/#, retrieved on August 17, 2020.

4 Jason Furman, *The concept of neutrality in tax policy*, available at: www.brookings.edu/wp-content/uploads/2016/06/0415_tax-_neutrality_furman-1.pdf, retrieved on April 14, 2020.

5 Antonio Calisto Pato, Cross-border direct tax issues of investment funds from the perspective of European law, *EC Tax Review*, 5, 2008.

emerged with the custom union, essentially a tax law concept, and evolved together with other topics of tax harmonization.

Still, the existence of the EU tax law is disputed[6] and it is described as the reflection of two characteristics that have negative impact on the proper functioning of the internal market. Firstly, the fact that an economic operation event could be taxed twice in the EU creates an important limitation for the free movement of people and their capital on the internal market. Secondly, the present miss-coordination of the corporate taxation in the Member States generates both obstacles and opportunities for companies operating within EU, as they face 27 different corporate tax bases, creating high operative costs and bureaucratic liabilities that are both limiting the European competitiveness and generating opportunities for aggressive tax-planning schemes based on the exploitation of mismatches.[7]

In the general context of globalization, digitalization and internationalization of the economy, taxation evolved from a national regulatory prerogative to a very demanding and intensely argued subject of cooperation among governments. The topic is acute and the difficulty in finding reasonable and efficient (if not perfect) regulation is generated by the dimension of divergent interests: paying less taxes and obtaining higher revenues to the state budget. It is generally acknowledged that the governments, which are competent in implementing money spending policy, are oriented to keep their offices for longer terms, so they prefer to gain the voters trust by proving their generosity in spending. Consequently, large public budgets can support bountiful public spending programs and generate higher electoral satisfaction. For sure, maximizing the public budget income is in direct connection with the respect for the liability to pay taxes and with the efficiency of the regulation of the tax system.

1.1 Current topics for research in taxation

Taxation is a topic of intensive research; scholars and practitioners are looking for the appropriate rules of law to limit and, if possible, to eradicate tax avoidance. Among the taxpayers, companies are more likely to adapt their activities, looking for the most innovative ways in saving tax money, especially when operating at the international level. The ubiquity of using state

6 Daniel Deak, Legal considerations of tax evasion and tax avoidance (September 12, 2009), *Society & Economy*, 26(1), 41–85, 2004, available at: https://ssrn.com/abstract=1472508

7 Paolo Arginelli, A proposal for harmonizing the rules on the allocation of taxing rights within the European Union and in relations with third countries, *Pistone Pasquale, Part 6 – A Possible Roadmap: European Tax Integration*, 653–694, 2018.

sovereign rights to rule taxation and the dysfunctions of the mechanism of international taxation create the opportunity for avoiding the tax mandatory liability. It is expected that a taxpayer uses all available methods to reduce fiscal payments, especially when its activity is flexible and innovative. This conduct is usually called tax planning and it is not unanimously qualified as illegal,[8] but its effects on the public budgets are negative in all cases.[9]

Weaknesses in the current domestic rules create opportunities for diminishing the amount of money that is subject to taxation (strategy called base erosion) and for moving the profits from one company, which is subject to high taxation, to another company in the same group that is situated in a territory with a lower level of taxation (which is called profit shifting). Usually, a precise taxation subject uses strategic tax planning, and it may take advantage of both these mechanisms, which are together addressed in literature and by practitioners as Base Erosion and Profit Shifting (BEPS). The dimension of tax avoidance using BEPS requires courageous measures adopted by policy makers to restore confidence in the taxation system and to ensure that profits are submitted to justified fiscal treatment, in respect of the fundamental principle of equity in taxation.

There are different levels of action in response to MNEs' efforts to identify methods for optimizing their fiscal liability. There is the national level, the most convenient one in terms of time reaction, effectiveness of the ruling procedure and administrative costs, but also less efficient for the taxation of the corporations' income generated in internationally developed economic activity. In this direction some countries (e.g. France's digital service tax) have already taken important and controversial steps.

There is also the regional level, for big states and for the local association of states (USA and EU) and there is the worldwide level, the most efficient in terms of intended results but the most sinuous in terms of adoption procedure. The analysis of the results generated by the tax reform at local and regional level is not encouraging for supporting this type of action,[10] the equality of taxation and the efficiency of the regulatory system being in

8 Simone de Colle and Anne Marie Bennett, State-induced, strategic or toxic? In ethical analysis of tax avoidance practices, *Business & Professional Ethics Journal*, 33(1), 53–82, 2014.

9 Kay Blaufus, Matthias Braune, Jochen Hundsdoerfer and Martin Jacob, *Does legality matter? The case of tax avoidance and evasion, arqus Discussion Paper*, No. 193, Berlin, Arbeitskreis Quantitative Steuerlehre (arqus), 2015.

10 Mihaela Tofan, *State right to rule tax system vis-à-vis multilateral regulation on new nexus and income allocation*, Cluj Tax Forum no. 7/2019, available at: https://heinonline.org/HOL/LandingPage?handle=hein.journals/cluj2019&div=50&id=&page=, retrieved on October 15, 2021.

direct dependency relation with the global acceptance of the new concepts and fiscal treatment.

The international regulation in the field is dominated by the Organisation for Economic Co-operation and Development's (OECD) actions in 2015[11] and 2019[12] and oriented by the 2017 changes in taxation by the US,[13] and it is accompanied by the EU's struggle to identify efficient methods to fight tax avoidance, in general, and BEPS, in particular by the end of 2020.[14]

The widest level of regulating the MNEs' taxation in the present context is supported by the Organisation for Economic Cooperation and Development's (OECD) initiatives to adopt a unified approach for international taxation. There is an intense debate on the proposed regulation; information was presented in documents for public comments and further analysis by specialists, researchers, and representatives of the MNEs during a meeting at the OECD headquarters.

The OECD's unified approach for fighting aggressive tax planning has two main pillars, and it was presented in January 2019, when the Inclusive Framework on BEPS has approved a Policy Note on Addressing the Tax Challenges of the Digitalisation of the Economy. The proposed directions for action envisaged the following:

- Pillar One addresses the allocation of taxing rights between jurisdictions and describes proposals for new profit allocation and nexus rules based on the concepts of "significant economic presence" and the exploitation of "user participation" and "marketing intangibles" in a jurisdiction.
- Pillar Two (also referred to as the "GloBE" proposal) calls for the development of a coordinated set of rules to address ongoing risks from

11 OECD, *Measuring and monitoring BEPS, action 11–2015 final report*, OECD/G20 Base Erosion and Profit Shifting Project, Paris, OECD Publishing, 2015, doi:10.1787/9789264241343-en.

12 OECD and country officials discussed OECD's workplan for new rules for taxing multinational businesses and ongoing projects in the annual tax conference in Washington, DC, on June 3–4, 2019. Under the name *The Road to 2020: Tax Challenges of Digitalization*, new proposal for Profit Allocation and Nexus (Pillar One) were analyzed (https://taxinsights.ey.com/archive/archive-news/oecd-and-country-officials-discuss-oecd-workplan-for-new-rules.aspx, retrieved on August 17, 2020).

13 Erica York and Alex Muresianu, *The tax cuts and jobs act simplified the tax filing process for millions of households*, Fiscal Fact No. 604, Washington, DC, Tax Foundation, 2018.

14 European Commission, *Aggressive tax planning indicators, final report*, TAXUD/2016/DE/319 FWC No. TAXUD/2015/CC/131, available at: https://ec.europa.eu/taxation_customs/sites/taxation/files/taxation_papers_71_atp_.pdf, retrieved on March 15, 2020.

structures that allow MNEs to shift profit to jurisdictions where they are subject to no or very low taxation.

Pillar One in the OECD proposal targets new profit allocation rules, based on the definition for the new nexus which includes:

- A positive approach: defining the companies within the scope
- A negative approach: not eliminating the presence on the market criterion

In other words, the new nexus is not about a sort of physical presence of any kind, but it is connected with the significance of the impact of the activity of some MNEs on a certain market jurisdiction. The physical presence, when it does occur, is a secondary criterion of analysis. The "Unified Approach" focuses on large consumer (including user) facing businesses and it includes two dimensions: the substantive and the procedural. From the substantive point of view, the proposal includes some definitions for the main used concepts, to bring certainty to the proposed regulation. The definition of the MNE group takes into consideration that its activity may include remote interaction and the multinational dimension of the company could be considered whenever either the owners, assets, clients, partners, and consumers location are in different jurisdictions. In my opinion, adding the jurisdictions where the "value creation" takes place might give a broader and welcoming approach to the concept.

The proposal addressed large consumers-facing businesses described in the regulatory text emphasizing the remote interaction element, applicable for all the types of the significant operations of the diverse businesses (production, service, marketing, branding, sales, types of remote operations, clients, partners, etc.). The definition of the MNE includes different business models, considering the consolidation aspect of income, from the economic point of view. To satisfy the generality and the simplicity of the proposal, the MNEs' definition in the proposal includes but it is not limited to the digital companies. The initial size limitation for the companies under the scope of the regulation was a €750 million revenue threshold used for country-by-country reporting requirements. This threshold raises important limitations and challenges for the developing and emerging economies that could benefit less from the provision of the proposed regulation. If the new regulation would keep its addressability to the big economies, the unilateral tax initiatives would be encouraged for the economic activities that do not reach the threshold and the new nexus, as a global provision, will fail to achieve its goals. As the proposal favors multilateral international taxation regulation, the unitary threshold approach might generate integrated global results, and not only using the quantitative precise perspective, also using the same method of determination. It is probably useful to note that the same level of the turnover is considered for the companies under the EU CC(C)TB proposal. Following this comparison path, the OECD proposal might notice the ambitious European proposal to reduce it to limit/eliminate the threshold after the first 7 years of implementation.[15]

The proposal states that the simplest way of operating the new rule would be to define a revenue threshold in the market as the primary indicator of a sustained and significant involvement in that jurisdiction. Some regulatory provisions should respond to the question of how the concepts of consumer products or consumer sales would deal with the supply of goods and services through intermediaries, the supply of component products and the use of franchise arrangements. The following the money rule could point out the real beneficiary of the operation. Although the proposal refers to the possibility of adapting the threshold in response to the different markets' size and structure.

The standalone rule of the new nexus, on top of the permanent establishment rule, is meant to limit any unintended spillover effect on other existing rules. To ensure neutrality for different business models, the level of applicability of the regulation would have to be general, capturing all forms of remote involvement in the economy of a market jurisdiction. For the general addressability of the regulation, it is useful to avoid/limit exceptions to the new nexus rule, so the proposal should be applied to groups that sell in a market through a distributor (whether a related or non-related local entity), whenever there is no double taxation scenario.

Under Pillar Two of the OECD Programme of Work, members of the Inclusive Framework agreed to explore, on a without prejudice basis, issues and design options in connection with the development of a coordinated set of rules entitled GloBE. The four component parts of the GloBE proposal are:

1 An income inclusion rule that would tax the income of a foreign branch or a controlled entity if that income was subject to tax at an effective rate that is below a minimum rate
2 An undertaxed payments rule that would operate by way of a denial of a deduction or imposition of source-based taxation (including withholding tax) for a payment to a related party if that payment was not subject to tax at or above a minimum rate

15 Mihaela Tofan, The challenges of the CCTB/CCCTB project: from harmonisation to tax integration in the European Union, *Cluj Tax Forum Journal*, 15, 2019, available at: https://heinonline.org/HOL/LandingPage?handle=hein.journals/cluj2019&div=17&id=&page=

3 c) A switch-over rule to be introduced into tax treaties that would permit a residence jurisdiction to switch from an exemption to a credit method where the profits attributable to a permanent establishment (PE) or derived from immovable property (which is not part of a PE) are subject to an effective rate below the minimum rate

4 d) A subject to tax rule that would complement the undertaxed payment rule by subjecting a payment to withholding or other taxes at source and adjusting eligibility for treaty benefits on certain items of income where the payment is not subject to tax at a minimum rate

These rules would be implemented by way of changes to domestic law and tax treaties and would incorporate a coordination or ordering rule to avoid the risk of double taxation that might otherwise arise where more than one jurisdiction seeks to apply these rules to the same structure or arrangement.

Like the proposal in Pillar One, the GloBE proposal under Pillar Two represents a substantial change to the international tax architecture. This Pillar seeks to comprehensively address remaining BEPS challenges by ensuring that the profits of internationally operating businesses are subject to a minimum rate of tax, reducing the incentive for taxpayers to engage in profit shifting and establishing a floor for tax competition among jurisdictions. In doing so, the GloBE proposal is intended to address the remaining BEPS challenges linked to the digitalization of the economy, but it goes even further and addresses these challenges more broadly. The GloBE proposal is expected to affect the behavior of taxpayers and jurisdictions, responding to the necessity that the global action is needed to stop a harmful race to the bottom on corporate taxes, which risks shifting the burden of taxes onto less mobile bases and may pose a particular risk for developing countries with small economies.

Depending on its design, the GloBE proposal may shield developing countries from pressure to offer inefficient tax incentives. The GloBE proposal is based on the premise that, in the absence of a coordinated and multilateral solution, there is a risk of uncoordinated, unilateral action, both to attract more tax base and to protect existing tax base, with adverse consequences for all jurisdictions. The GloBE proposal should be designed to achieve these objectives consistent with principles of design simplicity that will minimize compliance and administration costs and the risk of double taxation.

Considering the status of implementation of OECD's BEPS guidelines,[16] the perspectives of tax cooperation among states are justified, pointing out the transformation in the sovereignty concept globally and in the EU, in

16 OECD, *International collaboration to end tax avoidance*, available at: www.oecd.org/tax/beps/, retrieved on April 20, 2020.

particular. The EU Council's conclusions (2015)[17] stressed the need to find common and flexible solutions, consistent with OECD BEPS conclusions, and the Council Directive (EU) 2016/1164,[18] looking for proper rules to fight tax avoidance practices that directly affect the functioning of the internal market. The volatility of the regulation is even more present nowadays, when the global pandemic crises puts further stress on the public budgets. There is also the necessity to rebuild the trust in the legitimacy of the public budgets, not only in the spending procedure but also in collecting the income, with regard to the fundamental principle of taxing all the revenues from the economic activity.

On November 4, 2021, the statement which has been discussed in the OECD/G20 Inclusive Framework on BEPS was issued, noting that not all Inclusive Framework members have joined. The statement continued the two-pillar approach to formulate the practical Solution to Address the Tax Challenges Arising from the Digitalization of the Economy.[19] The precise rules of this statement are presented in Section 4.1 of this publication.

The topic is under ongoing debate in EU also, where the corporate tax reform package launched in 2016 has advanced very slowly, partially due to the global economic challenges and pressure in terms of pandemic crises and partially due to the lack of Member States' consensus.[20] The reform is meant to respond to the necessity to create a common consolidated corporate tax base, to draw a double taxation dispute resolution mechanism and to regulate hybrid mismatches with third countries. Two years after its launching, the European tax reform has extended its scope with the goal to identify efficient methods for fair taxation of the digital economy.[21]

17 *European Council conclusions*, adopted in the European Council meeting (March 19–20, 2015), www.consilium.europa.eu/media/21888/european-council-conclusions-19-20-march-2015-en.pdf, retrieved on July 1, 2020.

18 Council Directive (EU) 2016/1164 of July 12, 2016, laying down rules against tax avoidance practices that directly affect the functioning of the internal market, available at: https://eur-lex.europa.eu/legal-content/EN/TXT/PDF/?uri=CELEX:32016L1164&from=EN, retrieved on April 10, 2020.

19 *The statement on a two-pillar solution to address the tax challenges arising from the digitalisation of the economy*, October 8, 2021, available at: www.oecd.org/tax/beps/statement-on-a-two-pillar-solution-to-address-the-tax-challenges-arising-from-the-digitalisation-of-the-economy-october-2021.htm, retrieved on January 10, 2022.

20 Details about the corporate tax reform package, available at: https://ec.europa.eu/taxation_customs/corporate-tax-reform-package_en.

21 *The relation international taxation - international law: formal strains and jurisprudential effect*, EASTERN JOURNAL OF EUROPEAN STUDIES Volume 12, Issue 2, 2021, DOI: 10.47743/ejes-2021-0201, pp. 151–168.

1.2 Goals of the study and specific approach

The main research question here is whether solving the dispute among states over taxable income implies reshaping the sovereignty concept. Additionally, this research will establish what is more efficient: the traditional way of taxing using the sovereignty credentials or internationalization of the tax regulatory framework.

Almost 15 years ago, prof. Pasquale Pistone[22] tackled a similar topic by asking himself:

1. Which EU law limits Member States' actions, binding them to comply with it when applying their tax treaties
2. Whether tax treaties were (still) the appropriate means to regulate cross-border direct taxation issues within the EU and in relations with third countries

He answered these questions by proposing a European Communities (EC) Model Tax Treaty, which would have been compliant with article 293 of the Treaty on the European Community, as well as with the principles of subsidiarity and proportionality. Such a model, in fact, would have only steered the conclusion of bilateral tax treaties by Member States without requiring a direct intervention of the EU institutions in a non-harmonized area of law and without going beyond what is necessary in order to achieve the goal of better coordination of the Member States' policies in the field of direct taxation and avoiding the breach of primary EU law.[23] This proposal did not evolve to actual regulation, so the question is still justified and supported by additional queries.

As subsequent questions or secondary objectives of the research, the research investigates whether existing regulatory tools to limit/eliminate tax avoidance have already proved their general applicability and if their scope could be extended globally. Considering the argument that tax policy can support equity or efficiency but not both,[24] the research has as its subsequent

22 Michael Lang, Pasquale Pistone, Josef Schuch, Claus Staringer and Alfred Storck, *Corporate income taxation in Europe: the common consolidated corporate tax base (CCCTB) and third countries*, Cheltenham, Edward Elgar Publishing Limited, 2013, E-ISBN 978 1 78254 542 2.

23 Paolo Arginelli, A proposal for harmonizing the rules on the allocation of taxing rights within the European Union and in relations with third countries, *Pistone Pasquale, Part 6 – A Possible Roadmap: European Tax Integration*, 653–694, 2018.

24 Torben M. Andersen and Jonas Maibom, *The big trade-off between efficiency and equity – is it there?*, 2016, available at: www.nbs.rs/internet/latinica/90/90_9/TorbenAndersen_wp.pdf, retrieved on April 14, 2020.

objective to identify the effective tax avoidance regulation at national, European, and global levels.

Today's questions echo those formulated before, although they assume different shapes and justifications, due to the evolved economic and legal environment in which they arise. From a substantive perspective, the inquiry on whether (and why) there is any need to coordinate or to harmonize the regulation for allocating the taxing rights between Member States, on one side, and between Member States and third countries, on the other side, is actual. In the case of an affirmative answer, it is important to establish:

1 To what extent such rules should be coordinated or harmonized
2 What should be regarded as the most effective and efficient solutions

From a formal perspective, it is necessary to look for the appropriate legal instruments to implement the required coordination (or harmonization) and, in particular, to decide whether bilateral tax treaties should still be regarded as the most suitable means to achieve that result,[25] or a larger cooperation regulatory tool should be used.

Interest in the subject is growing for tax professionals and equally for non-specialists, as the evolution and development of the tax systems and tax avoidance regulation affect all subjects of law, individuals, and legal persons equally. The topics that we shall analyze are linked to the concept of fiscal sovereignty, the effects of recent major fiscal policy initiatives on the European Union and the Member States, and informal mechanisms to harmonize taxation.

The development of regulation in the field of taxation, due to unilateral initiatives of the states, at a European level, while analyzing the OECD proposals, is investigated. The issue of challenges for the contemporary taxation systems is presented in Chapter 3, establishing the present status of regulation and the conflicts arisen from the interconnectivity of the global economy. The concept of sovereignty in ruling taxation is analyzed and its particular features at EU level (3.1) and in the EU Member States (3.2.). The re-design of sovereignty in taxation is investigated in Section 4, as a result of the European integration, using doctrinal approach for tax cooperation (4.1) and tax competition (4.2) and jurisprudential approach for the internal market (4.3 and 4.4). The final part of the study (Section 5) synthesizes the

25 Paolo Arginelli, A proposal for harmonizing the rules on the allocation of taxing rights within the European Union and in relations with third countries, *Pistone Pasquale, Part 6 – A Possible Roadmap: European Tax Integration*, 653–694, 2018.

conclusions, and presents some limits of the research and future directions to follow in the research field.

If sovereignty equals taxation with the untouchable state right to decide completely autonomously on the public revenue and it is perceived as fundamental value for the tax systems, then we could reasonably hypothesize that the unilateral regulation in the tax field is the legitimate method to rule in current times. To investigate this assumption, there are various accepted methodologies or ways in legal research[26] and it is not uncommon that more than one methodology is employed in the course of completing a single research project. The taxation field indulges in a multidisciplinary approach from the methodological point of view (e.g., economic, statistic, legal). Tax avoidance is a large phenomenon, and it can be addressed from different perspectives: the subject of tax avoidance, the methods of doing it, the prejudicial parties, the dimension of the effect, etc. In this wide field of research, our analysis focuses on the conduct of the companies that operate internationally and that are simultaneously a subject of taxation for different public budgets. The research uses both doctrinal or black letter research[27] with case-law analyses and a comparative approach of the active regulation. To the extent that legal research goes beyond doctrinal inputs and takes a broader perspective encompassing some aspect of law in its social context, the socio-legal research is also utilized.

A complex system of methods and means of documenting is used for analyzing, comparing, synthesizing, deepening, and concluding specific information of tax systems and tax avoidance. The study of the relevant scientific literature is carried out by qualitative, comparative, and deduction analysis. The information thus collected is processed through comparative methods in order to synthesize arguments to support or to contradict our hypothesis parameters. Subsequently, the assumptions are subject to validation processes, mainly by the conclusions expressed in published case-law, applying critical analyses to specific situations. The documentation phase includes selection and organizing relevant categories of resources, data collection, and information processing. The main methods of investigation are theoretical research on specialized literature, empirical research, exploratory qualitative and primary quantitative data analysis, analyses and comparison of the courts of law solutions in taxation cases, non-contentious case study investigation, synthesis, and deduction.

26 Dawn Watkins and Mandy Burton, *Research Methods in Law*, e-book, 2nd ed., London, Taylor & Francis, 2017.

27 Terry Hutchinson and Nigel Duncan, Defining and describing what we do: doctrinal legal research, *Deakin Law Review*, 17(1), 2012.

The collection of data includes analysis of literature in the field, doctorate thesis, articles, using IT tools, and the printed format. The legislation in force and the newest standards, databases, and OECD documents were identified. The available data is selected and inventoried, using the most recent and relevant criteria. The documentation for the research, starting with the literature resources and the information available in the library (courses, academic papers, and study materials in companies' taxation field of regulation) is considered. The first stage of documenting was dedicated for research in the library, discussion and participating in working groups (colloquia and seminars). Deep analyses of the concepts, the differences, and similarities of the taxation are spotted in the present research. The objectives of the conclusions of the research are to summarize the guidelines of the literature, to monitor and to follow the achievement of the objectives, to identify the limits of the research and to state the future directions for investigation.

The methodology used combines methods of theoretical investigation, such as the theory of integrative legal consciousness,[28] together with specific legal methods, including formal method and comparative law approach. The regulation was addressed on three levels of investigation: from the domestic/unilateral point of view, to the EU level and globally. The good practices in fighting tax avoidance and the results and models used in the multi-state taxation were acknowledged. The research identified the results in combating tax evasion and limiting BEPS, the characteristics that bring autonomy and strength to this area of regulation. This research outlines the differences that may appear when considering the international dimension of the domestic taxation system, the fundamental principle of equity in taxation and the legitimacy of using tax avoidance mechanisms, if the law is not specifically forbidding them.

The analysis is not limited to academic research, comprising jurisprudential introspection. The Court of Justice of the European Union (CJEU) constantly argues its tax case-law solutions based on the equity in taxation principle. Without a doubt, there is more to comment on the European concept of inequity in taxation, than the equality among the subjects of the tax. The US doctrine uses mainly the concept of inequality of the taxation system, while considering the situations of lack of equity. The differences between the two approaches require doctrine and case-law examination, in order to determine if inequality in tax policy is equal to the lack of equity of the taxation system, and which one generates better results.

28 Karl E. Klare, Judicial deradicalization of the Wagner act and the origins of modern legal consciousness, 1937–1941, *Minnesota Law Review*, 1978, available at: https://scholarship.law.umn.edu/mlr/1732, retrieved on March 20, 2020.

2 The insight of the tax avoidance doctrine

Taxation is known as a dynamic, competitive, and multidisciplinary field of interest[1] for scholars, researchers and practitioners of law, economics, and public policies.[2] The present research on taxation trends at the global level, generally, and in the EU, particularly,[3] aims at identifying the actual means to overcome the restrictions derived from the connection between sovereignty and taxation methods for limiting/eliminating tax avoidance.[4] Mandatory rules, necessary for limiting base erosion and profit shifting, such as deductibility of interest, exit taxation, a general anti-abuse rule, controlled foreign company rules and rules to tackle hybrid mismatches are analyzed.[5] Also, the global minimum tax for business income is under the scope of this analysis.

This topic is relatively new[6] and part of ongoing academic disputes both for OECD countries and for the candidates.[7] The US academics have remarkable results in taxation research,[8] which outline the effect of tax

1 M. Heller, Globalization, the new economy, and the commodification of language and identity, *Journal of Sociolinguistics*, 7, 473–492, 2003.
2 Richard A. Posner, *Economic analysis of law*, 8th ed., New York, Aspen Publishers, 2011.
3 Mark P. Keightley and Jeffrey M. Stupak, *Corporate tax base erosion and profit shifting (BEPS): an examination of the data, congressional research data*, 2015, https://digital.library.unt.edu/ark:/67531/metadc816234/
4 Gregory Pun, Base erosion and profit shifting: how corporations use transfer pricing to avoid taxation, *Boston College International and Comparative Law Review*, 40(2), 2017.
5 Global Tax Alert, *Luxembourg publishes draft law implementing EU anti-tax avoidance directive*, EY, 2018, available at: https://www.ey.com/en_gl/tax-alerts/luxembourgs-parliament-adopts-draft-law-implementing-eu-anti-tax-avoidance-directive
6 Radu Bufan, *Treaty of tax law – vol. i general theory of taxation*, Bucharest, Hamangiu Publishing House, 2016.
7 Mihaela Tofan, *Tax law*, Bucharest, CH Beck Publishign House, 2016.
8 Daniel Shaviro, *Fixing U.S. international taxation,* Oxford, Oxford University Press, 2014.

DOI: 10.4324/9781003309970-2

evasion[9] and avoidance[10] through use of tax havens[11]; a number of proposals have been formulated,[12] results of the extensive research in the field carried out by scholars and practitioners.[13] It is legitimate to distinguish tax planning versus tax fraud,[14] considering the first is within the scope of the legal right to organize one's activity in order to maximize income and the latter occurs when the planning of the activity involves breaking the rule of law or abusive conduct.[15] Some authors contributed to the wholly artificial arrangements doctrine,[16] associating the loss of the Member State tax authority in fighting tax avoidance with the next logical step in the courts' free movement jurisprudence.

Regarding the legitimate justification of the tax avoidance conduct, the European doctrine is split in two groups:

- First group includes authors/researchers who consider that tax avoidance is illegal, and it is usually identical to tax evasion, being itself a conduct that is not in accordance with the spirit of law[17]
- The second group includes the ones considering that tax avoidance is permitted, as it is the result of the lack of clarity of law, so if the law is not precise in forbidding a conduct, that conduct is allowed[18]

9 Vanessa Williamson, *Paying taxes: understanding Americans' tax attitudes,* Doctoral dissertation, Harvard University, Graduate School of Arts & Sciences, Cambridge, 2015.

10 Patricia Brown, *OECD update*, STEP Miami 4th Annual Summit, Coral Gables, University of Miami School of Law, May 31, 2013.

11 H. David Rosenbloom, International tax policy: a view from the US, *Australian Law Review*, 41(3), 2012.

12 Avi-Yonah Reuven, International tax evasion: what can be done?, *American prospect Lonform*, 2016; see also Jane G. Gravelle, *Tax havens: international tax avoidance and evasion*, Ithaca, Cornell University ILR School DigitalCommons@ILR, 2015.

13 Mihir A. Desai and Dhammika Dharmapala, *Corporate tax avoidance and high powered incentives, economics working papers department of economics*, Mansfield, University of Connecticut, UCONN Library, 2004; see also Marise Cremona, Peter Hilpold, Nikos Schneider Lavranos, Stefan Staiger and Andreas R. Ziegler, *Reflections on the constitutionalisation of international economic law: liber amicorum for Ernst-Ulrich Petersmann*, Leiden, Martinus Nijhoff Publishers, 2014.

14 Ulrich Schreiber and Gregor Fuhrich, European group taxation-the role of exit taxes, *European Journal of Law and Economics*, 27, 257–274, 2009.

15 J.A. Morgan, Taxing the powerful, the rise of populism and the crisis in Europe: the case for the EU common consolidated corporate tax base, *International Politics*, 1–19, 2017, ISSN 1384–5748, doi: 10.1057/s41311-017-0052-x

16 Lilian V. Faulhaber, Sovereignty, integration and tax avoidance in the European Union: striking the proper balance, *Columbia Journal of Transnational Law*, 48, 177, 2009–2010, available at: https://scholarship.law.georgetown.edu/facpub/1838

17 Violeta Ruiz Almendral, Tax avoidance and the European court of justice: what is at stake for European general anti-avoidance rules?, *Intertax*, 33(12), 560–582, 2005.

18 Robert W. McGee, *The ethics of tax evasion – perspectives in theory and practice*, New York, Springer Science and Business Media, LLC 2012, doi:10.1007/978-1-4614-1287-8

The discussion is mainly derived from the regulation addressing the taxation of the Multinational Companies (MNEs) and/or Controlled Foreign Companies (CFCs), which were generally analyzed for their actions that fell within the scope of tax avoidance.[19] The fiscal conduct of the MNEs usually includes

1 Extended tax deferrals in the countries where companies are located, in the context of a global taxation system (e.g., US)
2 Or large tax avoidance, including mechanisms to target reduced effective tax rates from the perspective of the country where the business is located, when the taxation system has a territorial component (e.g., France) and worldwide exemptions for foreign-sourced income as a result of concluding tax treaties and/or the Parent-Subsidiary Directive (e.g., East European countries)

From the doctrinal point of view, the legal evolutionary paradigm at the interface of international law and EU law describes, in metaphor, the changing evolutionary relationship between the European and international law regimes as a "tale of romance and divorce."[20] The two systems of law departed during the 1950s and the separation grew with each treaty concluded among the Member States. The two finally separated as an effect of the revision of the European primary law by the Lisbon Treaty. In the taxation field, the administrative and judicial procedure enlarged this separation. Given the collateral effects of European integration on the symbiosis between taxation and democracy, teleological grounds for supranational income taxation are present.[21]

In the relevant literature, the principal purpose test (PPT) clause is discussed,[22] evaluating its ability to prevent access to treaty benefits in abusive situations.[23] Instead, income tax and its cross-border

19 Błażej Kuzniacki, *Tax avoidance through controlled foreign companies under European Union law with specific reference to poland, accounting, economics, and law: a convivium*, Berlin, de Gruyter, 2017.

20 Shafi U. Khan Niazi and Richard Krever, Romance and divorce between international law and EU law: implications for European competence of direct taxes, *Stanford Journal of International Law*, 53(2), 2017, ISSN: 0731–5082, Author/Editor: Stanford University, Publisher: Stanford University – School of Law.

21 Jussi Jaakkola, A democratic dilemma of European power to tax: reconstructing the symbiosis between taxation and democracy beyond the state?, *German Law Journal*, 20(5), 660–678, July 2019, doi:10.1017/glj.2019.55.

22 Michael McGowan, Andrew Thomson and Emma Hardwick, Preventing treaty abuse, *Tax Journal Insight and Analisys*, 2015, available at: www.taxjournal.com.

23 Denis Weber, The reasonableness test of the principal purpose test rule in OECD BEPS action 6 (tax treaty abuse) versus the EU principle of legal certainty and the EU abuse of law case law, *Erasmus Law Review*, 1, 2017.

complications have been considered, in a traditional manner, as an inalienable feature of national sovereignty. Still, there are opinions in favor of building the European tax union,[24] or in favor of creating the European unique tax.[25] The income tax regulation constitutes the core of the justification for the European politics in favor of a unique taxation system. The key question is whether the European Member States have the political agreement for the re-design of the primary sources of law, which have been drafted to protect the sovereignty in taxation. The doctrine investigates the inputs of the rulings of the Court of Justice of the European Union (CJEU) in the area of taxation, mainly when connected or colliding with the four fundamental freedoms of circulation. Given the huge budgetary impact of the Court's solution in the field of taxation, three different indicators (i.e., interpretation and use of general principles of EU law, limitation of the temporal effects of the judgment and the number of references for preliminary rulings), were used to conclude that the Court has not been affected by external factors in its solutions.[26] It is the result of the absolute independency of the CJEU judges in their activity and also the reflection of the high ethical, professional, and moral standards of the court members.

Tax systems, cornerstone of our societies, are dependent on enforcements as much as on policy. The selective application of taxes that gives priority to maximizing revenue and short-term efficiency fatally affects the neutrality and fairness of overall tax systems; there is a decrease in the long-term efficiency of these systems, which crucially undermines the rule of law by slowly corroding one of the core values on which our societies are based.[27] There are voices qualifying this moment in tax systems evolution as the proper one for advancing a constitutional model of regulating international taxation, debating on the possibility to reconcile the public authorities' initiatives with the pressure of the civil society and the opinion of the companies involved in cross-border activities (either multinational corporations, MNCs, or controlled foreign corporations, CFCs).[28]

24 Paolo Arginelli, A proposal for harmonizing the rules on the allocation of taxing rights within the European Union and in relations with third countries, *Pistone Pasquale, Part 6 – A Possible Roadmap: European Tax Integration*, 653–694, 2018.

25 Mihaela Tofan, Argument for ruling a unique European tax, *Journal of Modern Accounting and Auditing*, 7(10).

26 Katerina Pantazatou, Economic and political considerations of the court's case law post crisis: an exemple from tax law and the internal market, *CYELP*, 9, 77–118, 2013.

27 Rita de la Feria, Tax fraud and selective law enforcement, *Journal of Law ans Society*, 1–31, 2020, ISSN: 0263–323X.

28 Steven Dean, *A constitutional moment in cross-border taxation*, paper presented in Tax Policy Colloquium, NYU Law School, New York, August 25, 2020.

The model of taxation that is used in such a large market as the internal market of the European Union may use one of the following patterns:

- The regulation designs the prototype of European taxes, whose essential legal structure is defined directly by EU sources and becomes binding on Member States
- Or the European law determines the general principles and rules of tax regulation, which are intended to outline the legal framework governing national tax[29]

In both cases, tax neutrality should characterize the tax systems' requirement which translates into the obligation that it does not determine any limitation to the economic operators' decision in its current activity, for example, where to establish or where to invest.[30] Tax neutrality is a widely accepted concept in principle. In practice, however, tradeoffs between different concepts of neutrality and different goals can be difficult to resolve. But in several cases this concept can provide a useful way to cut through some of the debates about tax policy and identify a more economically efficient way to organize the tax system.[31]

The first category of tax model mentioned here is considered to be in connection to more complex and advanced forms of tax harmonization, which covers the entire system of tax and which, in any case, aims to define the key elements of the tax structure (taxpayers, tax base, tax rate, etc.). The second type of fiscal model is in direct connection to some particular forms of sectoral harmonization, which cover segments of the system of tax and do not aim at defining the fundamental structure of the tax or the basic aspects of the structure of taxation.[32] The first model is mainly found in the field of indirect taxation (as mentioned in previous paragraphs). Consequently, the tax literature qualified the value added tax, customs duties and (sometimes) excise duties as European taxes, in the sense that the legal framework of these taxes are effectively included in the legislation attributed to the EU institutions. The second taxation model can be seen especially in the field of direct taxation, where European harmonization covers limited aspects of fiscal system.

29 Pietro Boria, *Taxation in European Union*, 2nd ed., Cham, Switzerland, Springer International Publishing, 2017, ISBN 978-3-319-53918-8, ISBN 978-3-319-53919-5 (eBook), doi: 10.1007/978-3-319-53919-5, Library of Congress Control Number: 2017934921.

30 Cesar Garcia Novoa, Tax neutrality in the exercise of the right of establishment within the EU and the funding of companies, *Intertax*, 38, 2010.

31 Jason Furman, *The concept of neutrality in tax policy*, available at: www.brookings.edu/wp-content/uploads/2016/06/0415_tax-_neutrality_furman-1.pdf, retrieved on December 20, 2021.

32 Pietro Boria, *Taxation in European Union*, 2nd ed., Cham, Switzerland, Springer International Publishing, 2017, ISBN 978-3-319-53918-8, ISBN 978-3-319-53919-5 (eBook), doi: 10.1007/978-3-319-53919-5, Library of Congress Control Number: 2017934921.

3 Challenges for the contemporary taxation systems

A tax system is a set of rules, regulations, and procedures that

1. Defines what events or states of the world trigger tax liability (tax bases and rates)
2. Specifies who or what entity must remit that tax and when (remittance rules)
3. Details procedures for ensuring compliance, including information-reporting requirements, and the consequences (including penalties) of not remitting the legal liability in a timely fashion (enforcement rules)[1]

Even if we skip in-depth analysis of this definition, it is obvious that there are infinite ways and features that individualize tax systems, even in the rare situation when two or many of them are considered akin. In such a diverse landscape, it is frequently possible that a particular transaction gets under the scope of different tax systems, each of them claiming a piece of the revenue. International taxation is not only present but important for every fiscal administration.

In order to observe the international dimension of the taxation system, it is necessary to consider that the majority of the European countries describe their taxation system in the fiscal code, establishing the competence for local authorities to evaluate and to collect taxes for all the income obtained within the area of jurisdiction of that particular state. The activities within the scope of other state regulations or under the conflict of two/many different regulations, either involving a taxable person with another nationality/citizenship or the income generated from transactions with legal entities or natural persons over goods from a different country, are to be addressed

1 J. Slemrod and C. Gillitzer, Insights from a tax-systems perspective, *CESifo Economic Studies*, 60, 1–31, November 2013, doi:10.1093/cesifo/ift015.

DOI: 10.4324/9781003309970-3

under the terms of the mutual tax treaty/convention between two countries. The diagnosis of a particular case is more challenging when the fiscal regulation is frequently changing, as is the situation in the many countries, especially in Eastern Europe. It is reasonable to consider that the volatility of the tax regimes[2] generates no long-term predictability for the taxpayer fiscal optimal conduct and, if there is no predictability about tax liability, there is no interest for innovative tax planning. This is not the case, because both the substantial fiscal regulation and the tax procedure are sometimes on a random and, I might say, even chaotic path. This favors tax avoidance, and it is deconstructive for the collection of public revenue from taxes. It is the mission of the fiscal authorities to keep the efficient line of regulation, synchronizing their option for specific methods to collect more, with the available mechanisms to diminish aggressive tax planning.

Tax planning is considered in some research to be mainly tax avoidance,[3] and it is described as the operation of using active regulation to diminish tax payments, although it may be permitted in certain circumstances. As long as the actual taxpayer presents a valid economic reason for choosing a particular location for developing the activity and a justification for the legal form used for certain investment, the activity is considered legitimate tax planning. Not only scholars, but also the courts are in favor of the taxpayers, admitting the legality of their tax planning operations, if their decisions are not issued for the sole intention of avoiding taxes, but are economically justified. Therefore, taxpayers are allowed to manage their businesses in order to keep low tax liabilities, as long as their actions comply with the regulation in force.[4] Within these limits, tax planning is permitted and acknowledged, but when the taxpayer pushes the planning outside the legal framework, the conduct is sanctioned by fiscal regulation and, eventually, it could be prosecuted under criminal law. It is though important to draw the line between permitted tax planning and illegal tax avoidance, both in domestic and international regulation.

For instance, it is only natural that the taxpayer reacts to the state tendency of collecting more, using tax planning opportunities, especially when

2 P. Van den Noord, *Tax incentives and house price volatility in the euro area: theory and evidence*, OECD Economics Department Working Papers, No. 356, Paris, OECD Publishing, 2003, doi:0.1787/410243688730.

3 Ulrich Schreiber, *International company taxation: an introduction to the legal and economic principles*, Berlin, Heidelberg, Springer-Verlag, 2013, ISBN 978-3-642-36305-4, doi: 10.1007/978-3-642-36306-1.

4 Ulrich Schreiber, *International company taxation: an introduction to the legal and economic principles*, Berlin, Heidelberg, Springer-Verlag, 2013, ISBN 978-3-642-36305-4, doi: 10.1007/978-3-642-36306-1.

they are explicitly indicated by the regulation itself.[5] In many cases, regulation in force offers alternative options, e.g., choosing between a permanent establishment or a subsidiary in another country, thus choosing the favorable tax system and choosing between financing with equity or debt, in accordance with one of the methods that offers the best tax advantages. In both these situations, if the tax law permits tax planning, then it is a matter of regulating the mechanisms of the fiscal policy, which translates into reality the fiscal program of the ruling authorities.

3.1 Sovereignty in ruling taxation

Sovereignty is not just a legal concept, but also a characteristic of the state power that is undergoing important transformations worldwide, in general, and within the EU, in particular. Along with citizenship, sovereignty has changed its basic meaning together with the development of the EU.[6] The exercise of national tax sovereignty in an international legal framework characterized by the lack of coordination and harmonization of the rules on the allocation of taxing rights among EU Member States and between such states and third countries generates international disputes and political tensions.[7]

Sovereignty, the main characteristic of the state authority, is nowadays in direct connection with democracy and legitimacy of regulation process. In Western capitalist societies, the three decades after World War II saw a strong interconnection between income tax and democracy. On the one hand, the democratically representative political process was a precondition for the legitimacy of taxation. On the other hand, redistributive income taxation has improved the conditions for equal democratic participation by allocating resources and equalizing political power among citizens.[8]

The concept of sovereignty, once relatively uncontested, has recently become a major bone of contention within international law and international

5 There are multiple choices in accountancy and fiscal regulation inviting the taxpayer to opt for the most favoring one in order to pay less, like computation of the entire loss and accelerated depreciation instead of straight-line depreciation.

6 J.H.H. Weiler, *To be a European citizen – eros and civilization*, Working Paper Series in European Studies Special Edition, Spring 1998, available at: http://aei.pitt.edu/8990/1/weiler.pdf, retrieved on August 18, 2020.

7 Paolo Arginelli, A proposal for harmonizing the rules on the allocation of taxing rights within the European Union and in relations with third countries, *Pistone Pasquale, Part 6 – A Possible Roadmap: European Tax Integration*, 653–694, 2018.

8 Jussi Jaakkola, A democratic dilemma of European power to tax: reconstructing the symbiosis between taxation and democracy beyond the state?, *German Law Journal*, 20(5), 660–678, July 2019, doi:10.1017/glj.2019.55.

relations theory.[9] Instead of assuming that the concept of sovereignty has a timeless or universal meaning, more studies have focused on the changing meanings of this concept in a variety of historical and political contexts.[10]

From the fiscal point of view, the sovereign state is able to rule the tax system,[11] to establish tax liabilities, to collect taxes, to apply sanction when fiscal discipline is not respected and even to pardon certain fiscal liabilities, using amnesty acts. In the doctrine,[12] it is assumed that the defense of fiscal sovereignty on significant portions of national taxation is due to an axiological choice: by proper taxation, states choose to keep the constellation of values enshrined in the Constitutional Charters by anti-sovereignty attacks, thus avoiding equality and freedom, the protection of the social community and the promotion of civil transformation, fighting with the strong impetus of the market toward defining values and interests in accordance with the expectations and decisions of economic forces.

Fiscal sovereignty is considered an important asset for governments and they are not willing to transfer it in favor of the EU, slowing down the reinforcement of the integration process.

3.2 The right to rule taxation for the EU Member States

The EU is a wonderful economic integrated area for the 27 Member States, and it is a construction that functions, despite the challenges it was confronted with and the controversies it is constantly facing. One of these controversies is the success of the European currency, Euro and the function of the European Monetary Union (EMU) for 19 of the EU Member States, although the fiscal union does not go along with it, as it is supposed to in the traditional economic model of financial integration.[13] The Member States of the EU have come a long and fruitful way in coordinating their financial

9 Jens Bartelson, The concept of sovereignty revisited, *The European Journal of International Law*, 17(2), 463–474, 2006, doi: 10.1093/ejil/chl006

10 J. Bartelson, *A genealogy of sovereignty* (Cambridge Studies in International Relations), Cambridge, Cambridge University Press, 1995. doi:10.1017/CBO9780511586385

11 Barak Orbach, *Regulation: why and how the state regulates*, New York, Foundation Press, 2013.

12 Pietro Boria, *Taxation in European Union*, 2nd ed., Cham, Switzerland, Springer International Publishing, 2017, ISBN 978-3-319-53918-8, ISBN 978-3-319-53919-5 (eBook), doi: 10.1007/978-3-319-53919-5, Library of Congress Control Number: 2017934921.

13 Enrique G. Mendoza, Vincenzo Quadrini and Jose-Victor Rios-Rull, Financial integration, financial deepness and global imbalances, *Journal of Political Economy*, 117(3), 2009, available at: www.journals.uchicago.edu/doi/pdfplus/10.1086/599706?casa_token=v7rgCxMSa9MAAAAA%3AR2Zka5IV5jQjhONhL_VT49ZpiBfJoLB4x5L5-YMLGipLwBzwTUNyN7KuToSte-UmRHYX3ySuwfs&, retrieved on May 20, 2020.

policies, but after the global financial crisis constrains in 2008 a step back in the integration may be seen. The EU representatives struggled to reinforce the European financial integration but the differences among the Member States' taxation systems, the global crises (including the most recent, the COVID-19 pandemic) and the extraordinary context of BREXIT is negatively affecting the whole process.

In the EU, the existence of a deeply integrated internal market order for the Member States and the concomitant lack of profound income tax integration is surprising. Differential or sequential integration between market order and tax order has constituted fiscal interdependence between Member States: formal sovereignty to regulate income tax systems allows differences between national tax systems, while increased economic operations create the context for the most flexible economic actors to have the opportunity to relocate to the most favorable tax jurisdiction. The interconnection between income tax regulation and the rule of democracy in the Member States has not been affected by fiscal interdependence that is present on the internal market. The consequences of fiscal interdependence for Member States' tax system resides in connection both to the conditions prior to drafting tax regulation and to the taxing regulation itself and its abilities to strengthen democracy. Therefore, there have been opinions in the literature that the procedural – as well as substantive – essential of a national symbiosis between taxation and democracy is affected.[14]

Member States are subject to the effects of transnational policy, which may act in two basic ways. In the situation of tax externalities, it is possible that the tax bases migrate from the jurisdiction with more severe tax systems to another, where the tax liability is lower. In the situation of regulatory externalities, the Member States are confronted with the necessity to avoid the transfer of existing tax bases and, if possible, to attract revenues from activities abroad. Consequently, the states adjust their tax systems according to the tendencies of the mobile capital and the option of the corporations. In other words, Member States respond to the requirements of actors whose flexibility on the market has been influenced by the fiscal advantages of a certain location, in the context of the transnational economic order and who have consequently been given the option of judicial exits and entrances. In this conduct, states use a competitive regulatory process, which is alleged to have turned Keynesian welfare regimes into competition states.[15]

14 Jussi Jaakkola, A democratic dilemma of European power to tax: reconstructing the symbiosis between taxation and democracy beyond the state?, *German Law Journal*, 20(5), 660–678, July 2019, doi:10.1017/glj.2019.55

15 Jussi Jaakkola, A democratic dilemma of European power to tax: reconstructing the symbiosis between taxation and democracy beyond the state?, *German Law Journal*, 20(5), 660–678, July 2019, doi:10.1017/glj.2019.55

The asymmetric European integration[16] that has advanced trans-nationalization of cross-border market order but preserved income taxation under national political authority has established fiscal interdependence between Member States of the EU and exposed them to transnational regulatory effects.[17]

In accordance with the European primary law, the EU institutions conduct operations and activities in taxation areas in respect to the subsidiarity principle, acting only if the Member State is unable to resolve the problems effectively. Usually, the problems arise from the inadequate level of coordination for the tax systems of the EU Member States. According to Article 5 of the Treaty on European Union, the principle of the assurance of competence determines the limits of the competence of the Union and the principles of subsidiarity and proportionality limit the exercise of this competence. The Union shall act only within the limits of the powers conferred upon it by the Member States in the Treaty to attain the objectives set out therein and the competences not conferred upon the Union in the Treaty remain with the Member States.[18] It is the precise case of the competence to rule the fiscal system, which is yet one of the Member States' exclusive prerogatives.

The Treaty on the Functioning of the European Union (TFEU) defines the internal market as an area without internal frontiers in which the free movement of goods, persons, services, and capital is ensured (art. 26.2 TFEU). According to this forecast and for a true internal market, fiscal harmonization seems inevitable. This is especially true for income taxes, as international double taxation and international tax arbitrage have a strong impact on business and investment patterns. However, European legislation requires only a certain (but not complete) degree of harmonization of indirect taxes, in particular value added tax (Article 113 TFEU). Regarding income taxes, art. 115 TFEU provides the European Council with a mandate to issue directives concerning the approximation of laws affecting the functioning of the internal market, stating that the council shall act unanimously. Given the requirement of unanimity, income tax remains essentially an autonomous prerogative for Member States.[19]

16 J.V. Hagen and G.W. Hammond, Regional insurance against asymmetric shocks: an empirical study for the European Community, *The Manchester School*, 66, 331–353, 1998.

17 Jussi Jaakkola, A democratic dilemma of European power to tax: reconstructing the symbiosis between taxation and democracy beyond the state?, *German Law Journal*, 20(5), 660–678, July 2019, doi:10.1017/glj.2019.55

Mihaela Tofan, *The accession of Romanian to the European Monetary Union*, Munich, All Beck Publishing House, 2008, 315, ISBN ISBN 978–973–115–453–4.

18 Kyle Richard, Are all tax rulings state aid? Examining the European Commission recent state aid decisions, *Houston Business and Tax Law Journal*, XVIII, ISSN: 1543–2602.

19 Ulrich Schreiber and Gregor Fuhrich, European group taxation-the role of exit taxes, *European Journal of Law and Economics*, 27, 257–274, 2009.

It is also important to observe that the principle of unanimity, applicable when the Council has to decide on tax issues, shows the Member States prior options to maintain their possibility to act immediately and without limitation in situations that involve tax policy, expressing, at the same time, the option for limiting the role of the EU in this area.[20]

Regarding the nature of interdependence between internal market construction and fiscal integration in the EU, certain characteristics which define this process have been outlined. The guarantee of economic freedoms using judicial control mechanisms proves the deconstruction of the internally established public authority, namely in the situation when the power of states to impose taxes is discussed. When the exercise of state authority to rule taxation creates disadvantages for cross-border operations, excessive tax burdens will be waived because of the judicial control, for the reasoning of unjustified taxing power.[21]

Cross-border investment by investment funds is still surrounded by an aura of uncertainty, stemming from the lack of harmonization of direct taxation in the European Union and the consequences of discrepancies in the treatment of these investments by different EU Member States. Uncertainty about the tax treatment of this type of situation, coupled with its complexity and constant evolution (derived from continued competition in financial markets and the consistent creation of new investment "products"), especially in cross-border situations, tends to trigger tax issues that have not yet been analyzed, such as possible discrimination and restrictions on fundamental freedoms that may arise when such investments are cross-border, both on a fully EU scenario and in scenarios involving third countries.[22]

Another challenge that has been identified in current taxation is regulating the option for the source jurisdictions to impose limited source taxation on certain related party payments subject to tax below a minimum rate[23] The issue seems to concern less European tax authorities, where the concept used in connection to the quite urgent need to draw

20 Pietro Boria, *Taxation in European Union*, 2nd ed., Cham, Switzerland, Springer International Publishing, 2017, ISBN 978-3-319-53918-8, ISBN 978-3-319-53919-5 (eBook), doi: 10.1007/978-3-319-53919-5, Library of Congress Control Number: 2017934921.

21 Jussi Jaakkola, A democratic dilemma of European power to tax: reconstructing the symbiosis between taxation and democracy beyond the state?, *German Law Journal*, 20(5), 660–678, July 2019, doi:10.1017/glj.2019.55

22 Antonio Calisto Pato, Cross-border direct tax issues of investment funds from the perspective of European law, *EC Tax Review*, 5, 2008.

23 OECD/G20, Base erosion and profit shifting project, *Statement on a Two-Pillar Solution to Address the Tax Challenges Arising from the Digitalisation of the Economy*, October 8, 2021, available at: www.oecd.org/tax/beps/statement-on-a-two-pillar-solution-to-address-the-tax-challenges-arising-from-the-digitalisation-of-the-economy-october-2021.pdf, retrieved on January 24, 2022.

a proper regulatory framework for the income generated in digital areas of business is fair taxation. The efforts to harmonize the Member States' vision on this topic are supported by the proposal of two directives. On March 21, 2018, the European Commission proposed new rules to ensure that digital business activities are taxed in a fair and growth-friendly way in the EU, with respect to the Proposal for a Council directive laying down rules relating to the corporate taxation of a significant digital presence[24] and the Proposal for a Council directive on the common system of a digital services tax on revenues resulting from the provision of certain digital services.[25]

It is not easy to respect the rules of unique European market and simultaneously respect the sovereignty in taxation, especially if we think about the freedom of the market and the need of the legal person to expand their business in the most profitable area. This generates the need to align the regulation for all the company's activity, including the fiscal aspects. While the approximation of the corporate tax may be easily justified in order to facilitate the proper functioning of the internal market, the legislation has yet to be adopted unanimously. The unanimity in the Council is a difficult rule to comply with, in the EU 27. It is, on the one hand, constitutionally reasonable to protect the general legal basis of Article 115 TFEU with strict legislation to avoid any competence by the EU. On the other hand, it is also clear that this special legislative procedure contrasts sharply with the ordinary legislative procedure, which requires only a qualified majority vote (QMV), albeit with the consent of the European Parliament.[26] It is reasonable to estimate that the Member States are most unlikely to agree on anything, because their taxation systems differ considerably, and they have the tendency to protect their prerogatives.

The general rule provided by art. 115 TFEU (formerly Article 94 of the Maastricht Treaty and Article 100 of the Treaty of Rome), gives the Council the power to decide unanimously, after consulting the Parliament and the

24 Proposal for a COUNCIL DIRECTIVE laying down rules relating to the corporate taxation of a significant digital presence, available at: www.oecd.org/tax/beps/statement-on-a-two-pillar-solution-to-address-the-tax-challenges-arising-from-the-digitalisation-of-the-economy-october-2021.pdf, retrieved on December 20, 2021.

25 Proposal for a COUNCIL DIRECTIVE on the common system of a digital services tax on revenues resulting from the provision of certain digital services, available at: https://ec.europa.eu/taxation_customs/system/files/2018-03/proposal_common_system_digital_services_tax_21032018_en.pdf, retrieved on December 20, 2021.

26 Anna Sting, Company tax integration in the European Union during economic crisis – why and how?, *Erasmus Law Review*, 1, 2014, available at: www.erasmuslawreview.nl/; https://heinonline.org

Economic and Social Committee, on certain directives for the approximation of national laws, as the common market integration process develops.[27] Although this provision has led some to call for further tax integration beyond the national state, others have remained skeptical about the democratic legitimacy of Europeanized taxation.[28] In order to respect the principle of unanimity, any tax specifically targeting a cross-border transaction could be seen as an unlawful restriction; this broad understanding of the sphere of potential obstructive regulation on the internal market would indirectly suggest that the full harmonization of European tax rules and regulations is able to solve any misunderstanding between concurrent legislation of the states. As a result, Member States' performance in supporting the symbiosis between democracy and taxation has been eroded. But things did not move so far until now, although there is unlimited support for unrestricted regulation of free movement on the European market, both in terms of entry and exit transactions.

The CJEU has repeatedly stated that EU Member States have the power to regulate in the field of taxation. The assertion of the role of national parliaments in relation to a regulatory proposal at EU level, before the adoption of the normative act and in accordance with the requirements of the principles of subsidiarity and proportionality, can be achieved through the yellow card procedure.[29] For the legal exercise of state regulatory prerogatives, national parliaments may require a revision of a draft regulation and the European Commission is obliged to amend its proposal when at least 19 yellow cards (votes) are issued. This threshold is equal to 1/3 of the total votes available, as each of the 27 national parliaments holds two votes, and if there are two parliamentary chambers in a Member State, each chamber has one vote/yellow card allocated. If the number of yellow cards cast is insufficient to lead to a formal review but exceeds 12 cards, the proposal is deemed not to be welcome. This happened with the 2011 proposal, in response to the increased administrative burden that Member States' tax authorities will have to bear by maintaining several tax systems (namely the local income tax system, the CCTB system, and the CCCTB system). Interpretation of the results of the expressed cards can provide a broad perspective of the

27 Pietro Boria, *Taxation in European Union*, 2nd ed., Cham, Switzerland, Springer International Publishing, 2017, ISBN 978-3-319-53918-8, ISBN 978-3-319-53919-5 (eBook), doi: 10.1007/978-3-319-53919-5, Library of Congress Control Number: 2017934921.

28 Jussi Jaakkola, A democratic dilemma of European power to tax: reconstructing the symbiosis between taxation and democracy beyond the state?, *German Law Journal*, 20(5), 660–678, July 2019, doi:10.1017/glj.2019.55

29 Mihaela Tofan, The challenges in CCTB/CCCTB proposal: From sovereignty to fiscal harmonization within the EU, *Cluj Tax Forum Journal*, 5, 2019.

national support for the CC(C)TB project in the 2016 version, compared to the expressed cards against the 2011 European Commission proposal.

When assessing the restrictive nature of a regulation, it is necessary to compare similar operations: cross-border economic activity is compared to a fully domestic transaction in terms of its tax treatment and when a tax treatment is considered less favorable, the taxpayer suffers an objective disadvantage, with respect to a cross-border activity.[30] The value of harmonization does not necessarily apply in the same way as the other values set out in the primary law, but it requires the formation of a political consensus in the relevant EU institutions for the adoption of tax rules. When observing this value into practice, the principle of unanimity is needed to ensure the recognition of the fiscal sovereignty of each Member State.[31]

Still, there are situations when exercising its sovereign right in ruling taxation, the state may impose a legitimate restriction. For instance, when group taxation is addressed, most group tax regimes are applicable to group companies that are in the same country as the parent company, excluding foreign group companies from the tax group. Group taxation imperative rules are addressed to centrally controlled groups, when sharing a common business objective. Usually, group taxation is applicable if two conditions are fulfilled, addressing requirements in connection to the tax residence of the group members and their participation in shares, i.e.:

1 The affiliate companies are domestic corporations owned by a domestic parent
2 The subsidiaries are controlled by the parent; the control is assumed if the shareholding exceeds 50% or 75%[32]

Needless to say, in such a case, i.e., transfer of assets from a head office to its permanent establishment abroad, taxes should only be levied insofar as the exemption method applies between the state where the company resides and that of the permanent establishment. When the credit method is applied, insofar as assets are moved to the state of the permanent establishment, then consistency could only be achieved by obliging the state of the

30 Ulrich Schreiber and Gregor Fuhrich, European group taxation-the role of exit taxes, *European Journal of Law and Economics*, 27, 257–274, 2009.

31 Pietro Boria, *Taxation in European Union*, 2nd ed., Cham, Switzerland, Springer International Publishing, 2017, ISBN 978-3-319-53918-8, ISBN 978-3-319-53919-5 (eBook), doi: 10.1007/978-3-319-53919-5, Library of Congress Control Number: 2017934921.

32 Ulrich Schreiber, *International company taxation: an introduction to the legal and economic principles*, Berlin, Heidelberg, Springer-Verlag, 2013, ISBN 978-3-642-36305-4, doi: 10.1007/978-3-642-36306-1.

head office to keep record of the hidden reserves (difference between the fair market value of the assets at the time of the transfer and its historical cost) and by postponing the collection at the time such assets are sold. In both cases, either when assets are moved from the permanent establishment state or from the head office state, the state of departure will tax only capital gains accrued before the intra-company transfer was deemed to take place.[33]

Group taxation is ruled using different options. The analyses of the used possibilities to set out the tax system for group taxation shows that few states use the full consolidation of intra-group profits and losses in line with the terms of active financial accounting, so the groups are not treated as a single taxpayer. Most states have regulated tax regimes for groups, which take into account the additional revenues of the group members, weighting it in different manners. These methods are called group tax schemes and they are considering the transfer of taxable income from one member of the group to another. In practice, the following group taxation systems have been identified:

- Partially tax consolidated system, including aggregation systems, group relief system, and group contribution system; all of them do not fully consolidate the group's profits and losses
- Full tax consolidation systems (e.g., the Netherlands), which seek to tax the domestic group as a single economic unit[34]

For the taxpayer, the regulation of the integrated tax group for the calculation of the profit tax has the considerable advantage of consolidating the income and losses within the company and its subsidiaries, leading to an edifying end-result for the whole group and without complicated artifices to implement tax planning strategies. Without group taxation, corporate taxpayers are encouraged to use aggressive tax planning methods (division of companies or mergers) to group profits and losses between groups from very different economic activities, only for reasons of fiscal efficiency.[35]

33 Mario Tenore, The transfer of assets from a permanent establishment to its general enterprise in the light of European tax law, *International Tax Review Intertax*, 34(8–9), 2006.

34 Ulrich Schreiber, *International company taxation: an introduction to the legal and economic principles*, Berlin, Heidelberg, Springer-Verlag, 2013, ISBN 978-3-642-36305-4, doi: 10.1007/978-3-642-36306-1.

35 R. Dover, B. Ferrett B., D. Gravino, E. Jones and S. Merler, *Bringing transparency, coordination and convergence to corporate tax policies in the European Union, study by the European Parliament's Research Service and the European Commission – European Semester – Reducing aggressive tax planning*, 2015, available at: https://ec.europa.eu/info/

Until the issue is uniformly regulated at the EU level, the unilateral regulation is the within reach solution considered by the Member States to benefit from the group taxation advantages, among which is reducing the use of separate legal entities, without economic substance, for the purpose of tax evasion. For instance, Romania has adopted law no. 301/2021 establishing procedural criteria for group consolidated corporate tax,[36] observing the imperatives of the EU legal order.

Although the unilateral regulation is the easiest and the most rapid way to achieve a goal of fiscal policy, it is not productive for European integration. The most obvious solution to address the issues of legal basis and subsidiarity is an amendment to the Treaty that would create a more specific legal basis for tax harmonization in the EU. If there will be such a change in the EU taxation that would admit the possibility to take action using the ordinary legislative procedure, only a qualified majority in the Council would be needed to adopt tax legislation. In addition, depending on the type of competence that the EU would have assigned, exclusively or shared, the issue of subsidiarity would either be outdated (if it is exclusive) or it would not be such a problem (if it is shared). Even when competence was to be shared with the Member States, a specific legal base would not only make it easier for the Commission to justify its action, but rather a mandate under the Treaties as tax harmonization would become one of the objectives in the Treaty.[37]

Legal double taxation may be generated by multiple scenarios, including the simultaneous applicability of the rule of unlimited and limited tax liability and double residence. If, for example, a corporation has its registered office (place of incorporation) in Germany and its place of management in the United Kingdom, the corporation is subject to an unlimited tax liability in both countries. Limited liability may also lead to double taxation, for example when a Polish branch of a German corporation receives dividends from a US subsidiary and the corporation is both subject to a limited tax liability in the US and subject to Poland tax on dividends received, because those dividends are resulting from the activity carried out by the Polish branch. Overlapping tax bases due to conflicting determination of taxable income can also lead to double taxation. For example, the U.S. rules to

sites/info/files/file_import/european-semester_thematic-factsheet_curbing-agressive-tax-planning_ro.pdf, retrieved on November 12, 2020.

36 Law no. 301/2021, amending the Fiscal Code, available at: https://static.anaf.ro/static/10/Anaf/legislatie/L_301_2021.pdf, retrieved on January 20, 2022.

37 Anna Sting, Company tax integration in the European Union during economic crisis – why and how?, *Erasmus Law Review*, 1, 2014, available at: www.erasmuslawreview.nl/; https://heinonline.org

determine the profit of a German branch may differ from the respective German rules.[38]

There are pieces of regulation of the primary source of European law, such as art. 52 TFEU, which allows restrictions on the freedom of establishment, if there is a reason of public policy, security, or public health. Still, we observe that the justifications explicitly mentioned in the treaty are usually not applicable in regulation regarding taxes. As usual when the law is not directly applicable to certain situations, it is the mission of the CJEU to explain and characterize the possible situation within the scope of the regulation, addressing in its case-law the legitimate reason for limiting the general rule on restricting freedoms. According to the main rule of European law, the validity of a national tax rule depends on the following three conditions:

- The specific tax rule applies in a non-discriminatory manner
- The rule is justified by reasons of public interest
- The rule is proportionate

In its jurisprudence, the CJEU has accepted a few justifications for restrictions,[39] depending on criteria such as:

(i) Anti-avoidance rules are permitted on the grounds that ensuring effective fiscal supervision is a reason accepted in the public interest. The fight against tax evasion is, in principle, legitimate.
(ii) Coherence of tax regulation is a necessity. In general, coherence describes a situation in which several different tax rules are systematically linked. Those tax rules must be in a systematic context regarding the same taxpayer and the same tax.
(iii) Allocating the power to impose taxes on Member States requires that each state regulatory authority considers both profits and losses when exercising its tax rights. Otherwise, a balanced allocation of the power to impose taxes between Member States would be jeopardized. Therefore, taxpayers should not be free to choose where they are taxed.

Still in line with this analysis, the effects of Article 293 should be considered. The text was initially included in the Treaty establishing the European

38 Ulrich Schreiber, *International company taxation: an introduction to the legal and economic principles*, Berlin, Heidelberg, Springer-Verlag, 2013, ISBN 978-3-642-36305-4, doi: 10.1007/978-3-642-36306-1.
39 Ulrich Schreiber and Gregor Fuhrich, European group taxation-the role of exit taxes, *European Journal of Law and Economics*, 27, 257–274, 2009.

Community (article 220), and in the Amsterdam consolidated version, and it indicated that Member States are committed, to the extent that it is considered useful and/or benefiting to their nationals, to productive negotiations between each other, to reach mutual agreement on:

- Protection of citizens, their jobs, and guaranteeing the same rights as those granted by each state to its citizens
- The elimination of double taxation within the European internal market
- Reciprocal recognition of companies or firms within the reasoning of the second paragraph of Article 48, retention of legal personality when transferring the registered office to another country and when merging operations involve companies registered under the laws of different countries
- Minimization of administrative procedure for the mutual recognition and execution of the effects of court or tribunal decisions and arbitral awards

The text proves the fact that the integration project grew its reliance on European legal order, rather than trusting interstate treaties based on public international law, and an inherent growth in the European "federal" mandate to take wide-ranging actions to harmonize direct taxes in a single market during the post-repeal period is inevitable.[40] Article 293 categorized the necessity of negotiation with potential to affect the integration process among Member States into the previously presented four groups of arguments.

It is important to state that the conventions eventually concluded in the taxation field are not a part of the EU law, but they enhance the flexibility of the European project using legal instruments applicable only for the signatory parties. In theory, these conventions are under the scope of the international law, instead of EU law. Technically, because such agreements are not a part of the EU legal system, they may not be used or censored by EU institutions, not even by the CJEU.

Prioritizing their own sovereignty, no Member State has proposed transferring the right to rule direct taxation in favor of the EU institutions so far. Following this purpose, in the Lisbon Treaty the rule previously enunciated by art. 293 of the Maastricht Treaty (formerly Article 220 of the Treaty

40 Shafi U. Khan Niazi and Richard Krever, Romance and divorce between international law and EU law: implications for European competence od direct taxes, *Stanford Journal of International Law, no. 53*:2 2017, ISSN: 0731–5082, Author/Editor: Stanford University, Publisher: Stanford University – School of Law.

of Rome) which required negotiations between Member States to ensure the abolition of double taxation in the European Union, was abandoned. In essence, it means that the use of a thick network of bilateral (or multilateral) agreements between different Member States to resolve the issue of taxation of income generated in international transactions in the European Union must be ruled out. The general objective of harmonizing direct taxes and the specific objective of avoiding double taxation on the European market is a task within the competence of the EU bodies and institutions.[41]

The withdrawal of a regulation incorporating the solutions to cross-border barriers at Member State level happened simultaneously with the intensification of the discussions on the European model of fiscal federalism, which considers that an EU-wide mandate is needed to develop direct tax policies as an integral part of the policies for the proper functioning of the single market. However, the field of fiscal policy remains an important item on the agenda of national governments and therefore European fiscal competence continues to be surrounded by legal and political complexities.[42] The increased number of publications in the European tax literature on this repealed provision is in accordance with its status as the only explicit reference to direct taxes in the EU treaties, the primary sources of EU law. Our analysis supports the observance that the elimination of the only explicit reference to direct taxation in the EU primary law:

- Is in line with the actual and natural dependence of the European taxation on European order, rather than its connectivity with the international taxation
- Suggests wider powers to act at EU level against tax obstacles in the single market
- Enforces the concept of differentiated or flexible integration in tax legislation
- Limits the application of international law within EU boarders, in favor of the European specific jurisdiction, which has developed prodigiously in the last half of the century[43]

41 Pietro Boria, *Taxation in European Union*, 2nd ed., Cham, Switzerland, Springer International Publishing, 2017, ISBN 978-3-319-53918-8, ISBN 978-3-319-53919-5 (eBook), doi: 10.1007/978-3-319-53919-5, Library of Congress Control Number: 2017934921.

42 Shafi U. Khan Niazi and Richard Krever, Romance and divorce between international law and EU law: implications for European competence od direct taxes, *Stanford Journal of International Law, no. 53*:2 2017, ISSN: 0731–5082, Author/Editor: Stanford University, Publisher: Stanford University – School of Law.

43 Shafi U. Khan Niazi and Richard Krever, Romance and divorce between international law and EU law: implications for European competence od direct taxes, *Stanford Journal of*

Yet, the presumptive European fiscal union will mandatorily bring the direct taxation within the scope of the European primary law when the Member States will be ready to transfer, if not entirely at least partially, their sovereign right to rule taxation in favor of the European legislative institutions. Although this moment does not seem to be easy to predict, we can surely estimate that this is the direction the European legal order is developing in nowadays, if not by direct methods, then by using indirect mechanisms such as CJEU case-law.

International Law, no. 53:2 2017, ISSN: 0731–5082, Author/Editor: Stanford University, Publisher: Stanford University – School of Law.

4 European integration in taxation

Although the sovereignty in ruling taxation of the EU members states is guaranteed by the primary regulation, the evolution of the community law and the European integration generated a tight connection for the rule of law in the field of implementing fiscal policies.

The cooperation among the European states evolved in an unpredictable way from its beginning, when the economical declared purposes prevailed, to the actual status of *sui generis* integration. Professor J.H.H. Weiler has wonderfully characterized federalism in the EU: the EU is neither a confederation, nor a federation in the traditional sense of these words, but at the same time it has its own "brand of constitutional federalism."[1]

In organizing the internal relations of the EU Member States, taxation plays an important role, in direct connection to the market regulation. Prof. Graine de Burca presents the broader legal perspective and the political perspective on EU taxation,[2] confirming the analysis carried out in the previous subsections and showing that the fiscal sovereignty is still under the ruling competence of the Member States in the EU and it was not transferred to the EU. The direct result is that the tax union is only a future possibility, not yet a present reality. Still, we take into consideration that one of the directorates of the European Union is entitled Tax and Custom Union, which reminds us that the whole European cooperation was built on a fiscal ambitious project (custom union) and, at the same time, opens the floor for discussions on the possibility to create a true and functional tax union.

1 J.H.H. Weiler, Federalism and constitutionalism, Europe's Sonderweg, in *The federal vision: legitimacy and levels of governance in the United States and the European Union*, Oxford, Oxford University Press, 2001.

2 Craig, Paul De Burca, *Graine – EU law – texts, cases and material*, 5th ed., New York, Oxford University Press Inc., 2011.

DOI: 10.4324/9781003309970-4

Taxation may generate a positive or negative impact on economy[3] and its mechanisms may be regulated in a positive or negative manner. "*Positive taxation*" implies that the institutions of the European Union are able to regulate, independently, a tax system applicable within the union, as a result of the partial transfer of fiscal sovereignty from the national states.

Opposite from the "*positive taxation*," used when the legislation in force is active, legitimate and able to establish certain liabilities and procedure to follow, the "*negative taxation*" refers to limiting the fiscal sovereignty of another state, still a member of the EU. The adjustment of taxes to ensure single market functioning took place through negative integration. Instead of building positive supranational tax rules, the Court of Justice of the European Union (CJEU) and the Council sporadically banned certain tax arrangements, which were to be removed from national regulatory orders. Although the promotion of markets through tax consolidation has made national tax authorities subject to national tax orders, it still leaves Member States with some discretion. While few directives certainly prohibit specific tax arrangements that may not be supportive for the single market, the CJEU's judgments give Member States ample leeway to decide how to reconfigure their tax systems to eliminate the disadvantageous treatment of cross-border economic activities.[4] For instance, in the Judgment of the Case C-375/12, par. 63, the CJEU considered the national Court's case-law, competent to assess a domestic tax provision which distinguishes between taxpayers depending on the place where their capital is invested, namely if it is capable of being regarded as compatible with the Treaty provisions on the free movement of capital.[5]

More recently,[6] in the Judgment of the Case C-334/20, par. 5 CJEU specifically stated that to prevent tax evasion or avoidance, Member States may take measures to ensure that, in respect of the supply of goods or services

3 Michael Herb, No representation without taxation? Rents, development, and democracy, *Comparative Politics*, 37(3), 297–316, April 2005, published by: Ph.D. Program in Political Science of the City University of New York Stable, available at: www.jstor.org/stable/20072891

4 Jussi Jaakkola, A democratic dilemma of European power to tax: reconstructing the symbiosis between taxation and democracy beyond the state?, *German Law Journal*, 20(5), 660–678, July 2019, doi:10.1017/glj.2019.55

5 Judgment of the Court (Fifth Chamber) from March 13, 2014 in Case C-375/12, available at: https://curia.europa.eu/juris/document/document.jsf?text=company%2Btaxation&docid=149134&pageIndex=0&doclang=EN&mode=req&dir=&occ=first&part=1&cid=1368081#ctx1, retrieved on December 20, 2021.

6 Judgment of the Court (Seventh Chamber) from November 25, 2021 in Case C-334/20, available at: https://curia.europa.eu/juris/document/document.jsf?text=company%2Btaxation&docid=250047&pageIndex=0&doclang=EN&mode=req&dir=&occ=first&part=1&cid=1368081#ctx1, retrieved on December 20, 2021.

involving family or other close personal ties, management, ownership, membership, financial, or legal ties as defined by the Member State, the taxable amount is to be the open market value.

The legal system derived from EU sources of law is actually primarily influenced by the effects of "negative taxation": the rules of tax law in the treaties clearly indicate that the main objective set at European level is to identify constraints and conditions and, more generally, to limit the power to adopt regulation for the Member States, in favor of the EU specific institutions; still, there is a general desire to preserve the taxing power at the autonomous level of decision of the Member States, and not to transfer this particular regulatory competence at the central level of the decision making within the European Union.[7]

The "negative taxation,"[8] the original paradigm for the EU taxation, is presently considered a transitory phenomenon, which will be soon outdated by the constant changes in the paradigm of cooperation of the Member States, in line with the status of the European integration, which some authors have characterized as a form of incipient "federalization."[9]

In this context, the recent evolution of the European fiscal harmonization, when the negotiations for new regulation are longer and less productive, together with the powerful effects of the principle of non-discrimination and other principles that shape the rule of law on the European internal market, generate the conclusion that the "negative taxation" and the concept of the of fiscal sovereignty for the Member States are complementary in the European legal order, as they are constantly determining each other's scope and effects. It is not a mechanism specific to the federalism pattern, but it characterizes one more time the European status of integration and cooperation.

The European legal order is sui generis,[10] so it is not surprising that the European regulation in taxation evolved in a particular way. The novelty is the success of the European monetary project even though it is not supported by the corresponding evolution of the tax harmonization, so far.

7 Pietro Boria, *Taxation in European Union*, 2nd ed., Cham, Switzerland, Springer International Publishing, 2017, ISBN 978-3-319-53918-8, ISBN 978-3-319-53919-5 (eBook), doi: 10.1007/978-3-319-53919-5, Library of Congress Control Number: 2017934921.

8 Pietro Boria, *Taxation in European Union*, 2nd ed., Cham, Switzerland, Springer International Publishing, 2017, ISBN 978-3-319-53918-8, ISBN 978-3-319-53919-5 (eBook), doi: 10.1007/978-3-319-53919-5, Library of Congress Control Number: 2017934921.

9 Koen Lenaerts and Kathleen Gutman, "Federal common law" in the European Union: a comparative perspective from the United States, *American Journal of Comparative Law*, 54, 1–121, 2006, doi:10.1093/ajcl/54.1.1

10 Schütze Robert, Two-and-a-half ways of thinking about the European Union, *Politique européenne*, 3(53), 28–37, 2016, available at: www.cairn.info/revue-politique-europeenne-2016-3-page-28.htm

4.1 Tax cooperation within EU

Although obstructed by the unanimity rule in the primary European law, the tax cooperation in the EU is mandatory. This is another field of *sui generis* action in the European regulation and the need to understand it arises from the multiple effects that are generated. With the first steps of the integration process, European Union institutions were paying attention to the negative effect of the tax obstacles on the internal market, as taxes are known to be an important determinant of economic behavior.[11] The first three decades of the European Communities' existence have been marked by fiscal integration on two levels: the elimination of intra-Community customs duties and the approximation of indirect taxes have begun, while integrated income taxes have remained absent.[12] The fundamental free movement of good, persons, services, and capital collide continuously with the tax regulation, boosting tax cooperation within EU, despite the sovereign right of the states to rule taxation. For example, cross-border movements of goods and persons reflect the differences in the national tax burden, that may result from the articular regulation for the same fiscal treatment in different Member States.

In the second half of the last century, EU institutions and their representatives made efforts for tax harmonization, identifying direct taxation as the first possible target of this process and searching for a uniform model for the taxes that have common features in all Member States. Making these common taxes the uniform taxes in the community would consequently lead to the inapplicability of the special or atypical taxes of each State. This scenario is not in contradiction with the possibility to eliminate the domestic taxation instruments having an effect equivalent to the restriction of the common market.[13] In the Neumark Report of 1962,[14] the possibility of unifying the structure of Member States' tax systems has been ruled out, but the harmonization of direct taxation has been considered for its ability to

11 Servaas Van Thiel, The direct income tax case law of the European court of justice: past, trends and future developments, *Tax Law Review*, 62, 2008, ISSN: 0040–0041, Author/Editor: New York University School of Law, Publisher: Warren, Gorham & Lamont Series: Current periodical series, Language: English, Country of publication: United States of America.

12 Jussi Jaakkola, A democratic dilemma of European power to tax: reconstructing the symbiosis between taxation and democracy beyond the state?, *German Law Journal*, 20(5), 660–678, July 2019, doi:10.1017/glj.2019.55

13 Pietro Boria, *Taxation in European Union*, 2nd ed., Cham, Switzerland, Springer International Publishing, 2017, ISBN 978-3-319-53918-8, ISBN 978-3-319-53919-5 (eBook), doi: 10.1007/978-3-319-53919-5, Library of Congress Control Number: 2017934921.

14 Report of the Fiscal and Financial Committee (Neumark Report), 1962, available at: http://aei.pitt.edu/34508/1/A677.pdf, retrieved on March 3, 202o.

diminish incidental forms of double taxation. In particular, the hypothesis of a harmonized corporate tax was proposed and the approximation of laws in relation to the taxation of personal income was foreshadowed.[15]

Despite the obvious need for uniformity when regulating capital and corporate taxation, the harmonization of income tax systems at the European level remains just a plan. From a market integration perspective, the disparity of national systems was seen as a potential impediment to the functioning of the common market, as were non-harmonized indirect taxes. The acceptability of the alignment of advancing taxes on the market was, however, based on the condition that harmonization did not impede the ability of Member States to use taxation for their intended purposes.[16] Meanwhile, the applicability of harmonization to local taxes was excluded, because of the general principle of protection of the European market and because of their territorial addressability to a restricted community, and thus appear overall to be unsuitable to affect the general freedom of movement protected by the EU law.[17] Later, in the Memorandum on the harmonization of direct taxes in 1965 and 1966 with the Segre report,[18] the need to approximate the structure of direct taxation in the Member States, to eliminate differences in treatment between residents and non-residents, and to exclude forms of double taxation, so as to achieve a real European capital market, was emphasized.[19]

In 1970, the Werner Plan[20] has seen harmonization of direct taxes as a necessary step for the effective realization of an economic and monetary union; thus, a number of goals were formulated related to the approximation of direct taxation systems in different national laws, which seemed in accordance with the logic of the federal finance but did not generate

15 Pietro Boria, *Taxation in European Union*, 2nd ed., Cham, Switzerland, Springer International Publishing, 2017, ISBN 978-3-319-53918-8, ISBN 978-3-319-53919-5 (eBook), doi: 10.1007/978-3-319-53919-5, Library of Congress Control Number: 2017934921.

16 Jussi Jaakkola, A democratic dilemma of European power to tax: reconstructing the symbiosis between taxation and democracy beyond the state?, *German Law Journal*, 20(5), 660–678, July 2019, doi:10.1017/glj.2019.55

17 Pietro Boria, *Taxation in European Union*, 2nd ed., Cham, Switzerland, Springer International Publishing, 2017, ISBN 978-3-319-53918-8, ISBN 978-3-319-53919-5 (eBook), doi: 10.1007/978-3-319-53919-5, Library of Congress Control Number: 2017934921.

18 Claudio Segre, *The development of a European capital market*, Report of a Group of Experts appointed by the EEC Commission, 1966, available at: http://aei.pitt.edu/31823/, retrieved on March 1, 2020.

19 Pietro Boria, *Taxation in European Union*, 2nd ed., Cham, Switzerland, Springer International Publishing, 2017, ISBN 978-3-319-53918-8, ISBN 978-3-319-53919-5 (eBook), doi: 10.1007/978-3-319-53919-5, Library of Congress Control Number: 2017934921.

20 Report to the Council and the Commission on the realization by stages of the Economic and Monetary Union in the Community – Werne Report, 1970, available at: https://aei.pitt.edu/1002/1/monetary_werner_final.pdf, retrieved on March 2, 2020.

effective results. In the early 1980s, there was a change in the course of European tax integration, in order to align national tax systems with the rigor of the European single market, the fundamental principle for the EU legal order. Moreover, the adaptation of taxes to the requirements of the cross-border economic movement reflects the doctrinal feeling that taxation is an obstacle and a deterrent to market activities, which requires consolidation, both domestically and transnationally, in accordance with the principle of economic efficiency.[21] The topic was taken up in the debate on the establishment of a monetary union and the Delors Report in 1989[22] described the approximation (or at least coordination) of Member States' direct tax systems as a crucial step in the process of European integration. It has been made clear that the fiscal integration can be beneficial for the economic and monetary union for three main reasons, namely increased economic cohesion in the internal market, improved fiscal supervision, and better control of tax fraud and evasion.[23] Thus, the need to coordinate the regulation in tax area in order to fight tax evasion is quite old, although it did not generate solid objective results up till today.

Starting in the mid-1990s, income tax systems have been changing their regime in the European law order, occupying a position that cannot be limited to the status of an indirect regulatory effect of the four economic freedoms. While fiscal integration initially was designed to facilitate cross-border economic operations, integration has become more accurate by the tendency to limit or even eliminate the harmful consequences of the internal market order when using particular maneuvers of fiscal schemes such as the erosion of national tax bases and changing the profit allocation. It was proved that the free movement of the capital, in particular, has the ability to determine negative fiscal competition among Member States.

The previous philosophy of fiscal integration no longer keeps pace with the stages of economic integration reached by building the market. In this context, the European Union Council in its configuration for Economic and Financial Affairs (ECOFIN) has set up the Code of Conduct for corporate taxation, as the right institutional response to the erosion of tax bases and

21 Jussi Jaakkola, A democratic dilemma of European power to tax: reconstructing the symbiosis between taxation and democracy beyond the state?, *German Law Journal*, 20(5), 660–678, July 2019, doi:10.1017/glj.2019.55

22 Jacques Delors, *Report on economic and monetary union in the European Community*, presented (commonly called the delors plan or report) by committee for the study of economic and monetary union, EU Commission – working document, April 17, 1989, available at: http://aei.pitt.edu/1007/, retrieved on March 4, 2020.

23 Mihaela Tofan, *The accession of Romanian to the European monetary union*, Munich, All Beck Publishing House, 315, 2008, ISBN ISBN 978–973–115–453–4.

harmful tax competition (which will be widely addressed in the following section of the study). The proposal was to abolish national tax-based arrangements that favored some taxpayers with unwarranted benefits. The measure was simultaneous with the European Commission procedure for allowing the application of the state aid rules, which in fact raised the question of potential selective tax benefits. As both measures imply challenging tax interventions, they had the effect of protecting the national structure of the tax base: Member States preserved their right to tax or withhold tax, under the condition that the regulated tax treatment was applied without discrimination (without favoring certain taxpayers).

The first two directives on the subject of tax harmonization were issued in 1990, namely Directive no. 90/434 concerning the operations of corporate organization and Directive no. 90/435 relating to the treatment of dividends between parent and subsidiary companies. At the same time, a multilateral Convention between the Member States (Convention no. 90/436 on the arbitration procedure for the elimination of double taxation) was agreed.[24]

The process seemed to speed up for a short period of time and in 1992 the European Commission appointed the Ruding Committee,[25] with the precise mission to establish the goals of a specific program for the harmonization of direct taxes, aiming at establishing a uniform tax base and a scale for tax rates to be used for the fiscal treatment of the companies' benefits; also this regulation has targeted transparency of the fiscal incentives, when they were available for companies' investments. Contrary to the conclusions of the Ruding Committee, the EU institutions manifested strong reservations about tax harmonization, considering that it was not appropriate to interfere in the political needs of Member States at that stage of the European integration. After 13 years, new regulatory initiatives in the field of direct taxation have been launched, namely two directives on the tax discipline of intra-Community capital investment: Directive no. 2003/48 on the taxation of interest paid to non-resident individuals and Directive no. 2003/49 on the taxation of interest and royalties paid between companies belonging to the same group and resident in different Member States. At present, three decades later, the implementation of the proposals in these directives is lacking or insufficient regarding withholding tax on dividends, coordination of corporate tax, taxation of dividends, the approximation of tax rates and the

24 Pietro Boria, *Taxation in European Union*, 2nd ed., Cham, Switzerland, Springer International Publishing, 2017, ISBN 978-3-319-53918-8, ISBN 978-3-319-53919-5 (eBook), doi: 10.1007/978-3-319-53919-5, Library of Congress Control Number: 2017934921.

25 Onno Ruding, *Report of the committee of independent experts on company taxation*, Executive summary, March 1992, EU Commission – Working Document, available at: http://aei.pitt.edu/8702/, retrieved on March 5, 2020.

tax base, the determination of business income, the treatment of tax losses, the taxation of income for mobile EU workers.[26]

More sustained efforts against the measure to diminish the national income tax bases have been manifested following the financial crisis in 2008. The European Council has adopted a directive addressing the consequences of tax evasion, an important qualitative change in the nature of income tax integration, not forbidding certain concepts of the tax base but dictating the rules that should be incorporated into national law. In fact, it is a step toward the positive integration of Member States' tax systems.[27]

While the harmonization of tax regulation within EU is indefinitely delayed, the approximation of tax systems of the Member States was mandatory to provide performance and effectiveness of the integration project. The early stage of the process was designed by the Members States' mutual urge that the sequential steps of the internal market integration would not target the elimination of the differences between the national tax systems, in line with the formalism of the fiscal sovereignty of the states. Integration was built on the expectations of economic prosperity, which would arise from the unrestricted cooperation of national economies, influenced by tax regulation of the Member States, where the income was generated and submitted to the domestic fiscal treatment. The integration of the national market was not perceived opposite to the national state role to intervene in the economy unless the interventionism was obstructive to the superior goal of the internal market. Regarded from a wider international perspective, it was the experience of "embedded liberalism": the liberalization of the cross-border economic activity translated into the competing demand of nation states, when they value the power to maintain their de facto autonomy to pursue fiscal and social policies without external constraints. This legitimized the lack of European integration of income tax.[28]

The necessity to adopt harmonizing tax regulation, especially with regards to direct taxation, should be analyzed in line with the fundamental principle of subsidiarity; consequently, tax harmonization has to be built by European institutions only when the particularities of transactions or operations

26 Pietro Boria, *Taxation in European Union*, 2nd ed., Cham, Switzerland, Springer International Publishing, 2017, ISBN 978-3-319-53918-8, ISBN 978-3-319-53919-5 (eBook), doi: 10.1007/978-3-319-53919-5, Library of Congress Control Number: 2017934921.

27 Jussi Jaakkola, A democratic dilemma of European power to tax: reconstructing the symbiosis between taxation and democracy beyond the state?, *German Law Journal*, 20(5), 660–678, July 2019, doi:10.1017/glj.2019.55

28 Jussi Jaakkola, A democratic dilemma of European power to tax: reconstructing the symbiosis between taxation and democracy beyond the state?, *German Law Journal*, 20(5), 660–678, July 2019, doi:10.1017/glj.2019.55

carried out in European territories may effectively affect the proper functioning of the internal market; all other scenarios allow each Member State to regulate taxation at an internal level, based on its exclusive competence.[29]

Within EU law, direct tax harmonization did not develop constantly, in comparison with the indirect tax, mainly because of Member States' tax sovereignty. Still, the EU law order is built on the priority of the multilateral regulation over unilateral law (the precedence of the European law over the national law) and on the direct effect of the European law, every time when the European rules are clear, precise, and unconditional to be raised and argued by individuals in litigations presented to the national courts.

As discussed in previous sections, the Member States have kept large competences in tax regulation, preserving their prerogatives to rule both material and procedural features of their tax systems. Accordingly, the prevalence of the EU primary law determined the EU countries to take into account the two interrelated principles when ruling their tax system: the principle of subsidiarity and the principle of proportionality, fundamental values of the EU law and foundation of the mechanism that support integration process.[30] Particularities of these principles are synthesized in the protocol on the application of the principle of subsidiarity and proportionality, the updated version of which is the Annex II of the Lisbon Treaty. Limited only by these two principles, the Member States autonomously rule corporate taxation, making tax integration in the EU a remote scenario. It is unanimously admitted that the main legal obstacles the EU treaties pose for harmonization of company tax are shadowing the benefits of the Economic and Monetary Union, namely the unanimity requirement in the legal basis of Article 115 TFEU. The most recent debt crisis and the current global pandemic situation worsen the states' urge to restrain their fiscal sovereignty, so there should be other methods to further fiscal integration in the present political climate. There may be treaty changes, enhanced cooperation, approaches to applicable laws and also indirect harmonization through the new system of economic governance.[31]

Moreover, it seems very significant at a symbolic level that tax harmonization plays a very recessive role, compared to the principle of

29 Pietro Boria, *Taxation in European Union*, 2nd ed., Cham, Switzerland, Springer International Publishing, 2017, ISBN 978-3-319-53918-8, ISBN 978-3-319-53919-5 (eBook), doi: 10.1007/978-3-319-53919-5, Library of Congress Control Number: 2017934921.

30 Karina Ponomareva, Principles of subsidiarity and proportionality in European tax law, *Financial Law Review*, 10(2), 2018.

31 Anna Sting, Company tax integration in the European Union during economic crisis – why and how?, *Erasmus Law Review*, 1, 2014, available at: www.erasmuslawreview.nl/; https://heinonline.org

non-discrimination and other general values of EU law, proving itself to be a less binding value and sometimes purely formal or programmatic.[32]

First, tax harmonization cannot be implemented directly only through legal interpretation because it is based on the existence of the support provided by secondary legislation. Contrary to the other European law fundamental principles (non-discrimination, the interdiction to affect the EU internal market freedom, the abolition of the customs barriers, the limitation of state aid, etc.) tax harmonization cannot be used by Member States and EU institutions in a direct manner, to justify their decisions, and it cannot be used by the courts of law when solving a particular case. Tax harmonization can be used only if there is a previously described model, imposed through a legislative secondary instrument (directive or regulation) that expresses the options accepted in the specific discipline of a harmonized tax.[33]

Eventually, a possible non-EU option may be considered, if we think that most of the EU Member States are also OECD members,[34] so multilateral agreements on tax issues are possible in this context. However, this research shows that the current EU legislative framework and the EU economic governance system led to achieving a more subtle and less intrusive tax harmonization, in comparison with treaty amendment that would increase legitimately and integration in the field of taxation. In exercising their powers of taxation, Member States have continued to rely on OECD principles, which aim primarily at allocating tax jurisdiction between states and avoiding double taxation, without necessarily including the free movement and guarantees of non-discrimination required in the EU's in-depth process of economic integration.[35] At the same time, for more than two decades, the field of research and the regulation on taxation is reforming in all the recent members of the EU, including Romania. The Eastern European countries constantly adopt new regulation in taxation area and some of them (Estonia, Latvia, Lithuania, Slovakia, and Slovenia) have already entered

32 Pietro Boria, *Taxation in European Union*, 2nd ed., Cham, Switzerland, Springer International Publishing, 2017, ISBN 978-3-319-53918-8, ISBN 978-3-319-53919-5 (eBook), doi: 10.1007/978-3-319-53919-5, Library of Congress Control Number: 2017934921.

33 Pietro Boria, *Taxation in European Union*, 2nd ed., Cham, Switzerland, Springer International Publishing, 2017, ISBN 978-3-319-53918-8, ISBN 978-3-319-53919-5 (eBook), doi: 10.1007/978-3-319-53919-5, Library of Congress Control Number: 2017934921.

34 The list of OECD members is available at: www.oecd.org/about/document/list-oecd-member-countries.htm; 22 of the EU Member States are currently members of the OECD.

35 Servaas Van Thiel, The direct income tax case law of the European court of justice: past, trends and future developments, *Tax Law Review*, 62, 2008, ISSN: 0040–0041, Author/Editor: New York University School of Law, Publisher: Warren, Gorham & Lamont Series: Current periodical series, Language: English, Country of publication: United States of America.

the European Monetary Union (EMU), while the others (i.e., Romania, Hungary and Bulgaria) are candidate countries.

Second, at the end of the political decision-making process, three income tax directives have been adopted to remove impediments to cross-border business activities. From a technical point of view, the directives postponed the corporate restructuring tax, eliminated the chain tax on corporate dividends, and canceled the source taxation of intra-group interest and royalty payments.[36] When performing a deeper analysis, it is revealed that the directions to favor direct tax harmonization used by the EU institutions mainly targeted the field of the transfer of the revenue in cross-border transactions, implying at least two of the Member States. Legislation on the approximation of direct taxation of income streams remaining in the single territory of a Member State did not have positive results and therefore it remained at the stage of simple proposal.[37]

We observe that more than half a century of European integration was not long enough to build tax integration; the corporate tax treatment, the taxation of the residents' income, and other types of fiscal liability are still regulated by unilateral intervention of the Member States, and in cross-border activities, the provisions of the tax treaties concluded by the taxpayer's state of residence are incident. Recently, the European institutions have promoted the ongoing corporate tax reform to fight tax avoidance,[38] an effort which includes various methods of strengthening integration. We shall address in Section 4.4. the proposal for CC(C)TB[39] and the fairy taxation of digital income,[40] which are corresponding to the OECD action presented in the Statement on a Two-Pillar Solution to Address the Tax Challenges Arising From the Digitalisation of the Economy.[41]

36 Jussi Jaakkola, A democratic dilemma of European power to tax: reconstructing the symbiosis between taxation and democracy beyond the state?, *German Law Journal*, 20(5), 660–678, July 2019, doi:10.1017/glj.2019.55

37 Pietro Boria, *Taxation in European Union*, 2nd ed., Cham, Switzerland, Springer International Publishing, 2017, ISBN 978-3-319-53918-8, ISBN 978-3-319-53919-5 (eBook), doi: 10.1007/978-3-319-53919-5, Library of Congress Control Number: 2017934921.

38 European Commission proposals to address Corporate Tax Reform Package are available at: https://ec.europa.eu/taxation_customs/corporate-tax-reform-package_en, retrieved on December 20, 2021.

39 European Commission proposals to address Common Consolidated Corporate Tax Base (CCCTB) are available at: https://ec.europa.eu/taxation_customs/common-consolidated-corporate-tax-base-ccctb_en,, retrieved on December 20, 2021.

40 European Commission proposals to address Fair Taxation of the Digital Economy are available at: https://ec.europa.eu/taxation_customs/fair-taxation-digital-economy_en, retrieved on December 20, 2021.

41 OECD, *Statement on a two-pillar solution to address the tax challenges arising from the digitalisation of the economy*, 2021, available at: www.oecd.org/tax/beps/statement-on-a-

4.2 Harmful tax competition

For many years, the topic of "harmful tax competition" has been one of the main justifications used by international actors, EU included, when evaluating and arguing the legitimacy of a state's decisions toward tax systems, in relation to their strategic development goals, and even to the peaceful coexistence of states in an international context.[42]

This leads to the additional problem of whether Member States have the power to introduce protectionist measures to cross-border activities (obstacles to free movement) whenever the tax disparity between them amounts to "harmful tax competition," as defined by the OECD and the EU in their respective statements on this issue. The application of any anti-abuse doctrine or provision is subject to the institutional framework of the EU and the extreme concept of "harmful tax competition" has been addressed either by application of Community State Aid rules or by political consensus in the form of "soft law" i.e., the "Code of Conduct" in 1997.[43]

Today, the fiscal sovereignty of the EU Member States seems to be guarded from a selfish position, aimed at keeping the autonomy of governments to decide their fiscal policy, while competing on the free market. Competition is not harmful in itself, economic theory proving its genuine results and long-term benefits. Still, in the particular context of the European integration, the fiscal competition comes in conflict with primary rules of law, such as the free movement of goods and capital, generating harmful results.

In fact, the multinational companies are designing tax planning strategies to reduce their overall tax liability and tax payments, speculating every possible advantage and technicality of tax systems, and significantly improving their final benefits. From this perspective, the definition of fiscal policies with an emphasis on territorial facilitation, aiming in particular at promoting the location of economic activities or capital investments in the country, was considered the expression of the "harmful" choices of globalization processes and therefore the element of countering or at least restricting European integration. Thus, some forms of aligning the fiscal policies of

two-pillar-solution-to-address-the-tax-challenges-arising-from-the-digitalisation-of-the-economy-october-2021.htm, retrieved on October 15, 2021.

42 Pietro Boria, *Taxation in European Union*, 2nd ed., Cham, Switzerland, Springer International Publishing, 2017, ISBN 978-3-319-53918-8, ISBN 978-3-319-53919-5 (eBook), doi: 10.1007/978-3-319-53919-5, Library of Congress Control Number: 2017934921.

43 Wolfgang Schoen, *Abuse of rights and European tax law*, available at: www.cambridge.org/core, retrieved on July 23, 2020.

each state are promoted by international organizations, in order to reduce fiscal competition between states.[44] Considering these arguments, the situations when EU, using its institutional mechanisms, is authorized to act in a tax case are designated by:

- The principle of empowerment, namely the EU must be competent to act in the situation that is analyzed
- The principle of subsidiarity, i.e., the delimitation of competence between the EU and the Member States is designed by the criterion of action which is best compliant with the objectives provided by the EU primary law (namely, its constituent treaties)
- The principle of proportionality, stating that the content and the form of the action do not exceed the limits necessary to achieve the established goals[45]

Harmful fiscal competition within EU is manifested in concurrence with disrespect to EU state aid rules. The regulation of EU state aid was adopted to serve a double scope: to eliminate the unjustified spending of public resources by inefficient fiscal incentives, consequently offering to the Member States the support needed to properly manage the public budgets and to eliminate inefficient private investment by preserving the competition on the internal market. Since 1998, the Commission has been applying the ban on state aid for tax reductions, policy implemented as a result of an intensive process to gain Member States' support. The dissemination of the state aid European policy was based on soft law instruments, such as notifications, recommendation, informative correspondence and other non-binding documents, which describe the application of the EU state aid ban to direct corporate taxation as necessary to promote good governance, to fight tax harmful competition and tax avoidance. The Commission's commitment to monitor the state aid in the form of fiscal measures is part of the wider objective of clarifying and strengthening the application of state aid rules to reduce distortions of competition in the single market.[46]

Harmful and limited competition is not permitted within EU, a rule included in the conclusions of the Council of Ministers of Economy and

44 Pietro Boria, *Taxation in European Union*, 2nd ed., Cham, Switzerland, Springer International Publishing, 2017, ISBN 978-3-319-53918-8, ISBN 978-3-319-53919-5 (eBook), doi: 10.1007/978-3-319-53919-5, Library of Congress Control Number: 2017934921.

45 Kyle Richard, Are all tax rulings state aid? Examining the European Commission recent state aid decisions, *Houston Business and Tax Law Journal*, XVIII, ISSN: 1543–2602.

46 Kristina Povazanova and Hana Kovacikova, Multinational tax avoidance vs. European Commission, *Bratislava Law Review*, 1, 2017.

Finance (ECOFIN) of December 1, 1997, when the Code of Conduct for corporate taxation was issued. The Code is not a legally binding instrument, but given its adoption procedure, it clearly has political force. The representatives of the Member States agreed to repeal the existing tax measures which constitute harmful tax competition and to refrain from introducing such measures in the future (conduct designated with the term "standstill position"). It is not only a declarative document, as it proposed the criteria to be used when evaluating any presumptive harmful unilateral decision. The typical expression of the fight against harmful tax competition in the "Code of Conduct" was designed to achieve new favorable fiscal measures, in order to promote the gradual dismantling of existing tax regulations, dedicated to encouraging the location of economic activities in a country, capable of producing competitive situations compared to other countries.[47]

The rules set out in the Code of Conduct have succeeded in achieving and effectively enforcing the value of harmful tax competition in the EU legal order. Starting March 1998, the Code of Conduct Group has extended its scope of activity with the mission of observing standstill conduct of the Member States and consequently reporting its conclusions to the Council. The Code of Conduct Group's main results had an impact on the rules, fiscal information exchange between tax authorities and transfer pricing transparency, administrative procedures and expanding the effect of promotion of European rules in third countries (non-EU countries). Still, the European Commission is competent to organize the whole process for the precise application of the EU state aid rules, and for this purpose it undertakes the mission to prepare and to draw up guidelines on the application of Articles 92 and 93 of the EC Treaty (Article 107 and 108 TFEU).

In order to explain the measures relating to direct business taxation, when adopting the Code of Conduct, transparency in the field of taxation was implemented through information an exchange system between Member States and the assessment of all tax measures that could be covered by it; the Commission argued that the EU state aid rules will also contribute, through their own mechanism, to the objective of tackling harmful tax competition.[48] In a different manner from the OECD report on harmful tax competition, the European Code of Conduct is not mainly focused at fighting

47 Pietro Boria, *Taxation in European Union*, 2nd ed., Cham, Switzerland, Springer International Publishing, 2017, ISBN 978-3-319-53918-8, ISBN 978-3-319-53919-5 (eBook), doi: 10.1007/978-3-319-53919-5, Library of Congress Control Number: 2017934921.

48 Kristina Povazanova and Hana Kovacikova, Multinational tax avoidance vs. European Commission, *Bratislava Law Review*, 1, 2017.

the relocation of financial assets or business that could generate costs for the company, consequently diminishing the corporate tax base in the state where the enterprise developed its main economic activity. It rather concentrated its action on the measures to expose the reasoning of the incorporation of the company in the territory with a relaxed tax regime. The code of conduct is usually in contrast to tax practices that can result in substantial benefits, so that the company's allocation options change in a different area than usual (or where the main economic activity is expressed).[49]

There is no doubt that in the European context the sanctions for unlawful tax conduct may cumulate administrative and criminal features, without any restriction imposed by the *non bis in idem* liability doctrine.[50] The investigations carried out by European Commission are the administrative procedure to generate possible sanctions for unlawful tax conduct.[51] The affair known as "Luxembourg Leaks" contributed to the development of EU state aid prohibition in relation to tax matters.[52] In 2014, the European Commission

49 Pietro Boria, *Taxation in European Union*, 2nd ed., Cham, Switzerland, Springer International Publishing, 2017, ISBN 978-3-319-53918-8, ISBN 978-3-319-53919-5 (eBook), doi: 10.1007/978-3-319-53919-5, Library of Congress Control Number: 2017934921.

50 As it has been pointed out repeatedly in Lolito Fedele's the contribution (S. Lotito Fedele, The Ne Bis In idem principle in tax law: European and Italian frameworks, *Central European Public Administration Review*, 18(1), 51–68, 2020, available at: https://orcid.org/0000-0003-0108-9863), there is no lack of ambiguity about that. In fact, contradicting the Advocate General's requests in the Menci case the European Court of Justice has recently admitted the cumulation of criminal and administrative sanctions for failure to pay withholding taxes (Article 10-bis of Legislative Decree 74/2000 and Article 13 of Legislative Decree 471/1997), limiting itself to stating that it is legitimate to the extent that there is "coordination aimed at reducing to what is strictly necessary the additional burden that such cumulation entails for the parties concerned."

51 Also in Lolito Fedele's the contribution (S. Lotito Fedele, The Ne Bis In idem principle in tax law: European and Italian frameworks, *Central European Public Administration Review*, 18(1), 51–68, 2020, available at: https://orcid.org/0000-0003-0108-9863), has been stated that such an approach would also be consistent with the requests coming from the neighboring area of European Union law – in which it has been argued that the prohibition of ne bis in idem enshrined in Article 50 of the Charter of Fundamental Rights of the European Union – is also valid concerning the sanctions formally called tax sanctions but which are endowed in substance with such a function as to assimilate them to criminal ones.

52 Hundreds of tax rulings of the Luxembourg tax authorities were made available for public. According to these rulings, the Luxembourg tax authorities helped multinational companies to avoid payment of taxes in other jurisdictions by granting beneficial tax treatments. The European Commission press releases said this could constitute a prohibited state aid but, in consideration of the Member States' sensitivity toward the regulation for taxing the revenues, the Commission presented its actions as an effort to combat corporate tax avoidance that exploits disparities in the tax policies of the Member States.

started investigations which received the mission to examine the in-depth situation in which three decisions were issued by tax authorities in Ireland, Netherlands, and Luxembourg, targeting the liability to pay tax on the profit obtained by Apple, Starbucks, and Fiat Finance and Trade. The questions raised were quite similar, regarding whether the proper respect was paid to the EU regulation banning state aid. Furthermore, on October 7, 2014, the Commission opened another thorough investigation on whether the decision of the Luxembourg tax authorities regarding the profit tax that Amazon has to pay in Luxembourg complies with EU state aid rules.[53] At the same time, the enterprises that have benefited from these advantageous tax rulings or other special tax measures are advised to prepare for the possibility that tax benefits resulting from their tax planning at EU level might be unlawful state aid and therefore they might have to expand their fiscal liability. From a wider perspective, the companies are obliged to take account not only of the applicable tax rules as part of their global tax planning and negotiation of tax rulings, but also of potential state aid considerations.[54]

On August 30, 2016, the European Commission ordered Ireland to collect approximately 13 billion euro from Apple Group, through its subsidiaries Apple Sales International (ASI) and Apple Operations Europe International (AOE). The amount in question described one of the biggest tax controversies on record and generated a lot of pressure on the decisions makers.[55]

Prior to the commencement of the challenged decisions, the US Senate and the International Consortium of Investigative journalists opened separate investigations into the tax practices of multinational enterprises. The Commission investigations were opened shortly after the US Senate hearings and LuxLeaks scandal, and the targets of these investigations are

53 All four cases concern tax rulings dealing with transfer pricing arrangements between entities of the same corporate group, which the European Commission has investigated on the assumption of illegal state aid. After three months of in-depth examinations, the Commission's report concluded that Luxembourg has granted tax advantages to Fiat's financing company, similar to the Netherlands for Starbucks' coffee roasting company. A tax ruling delivered by the national tax authority allowed the companies concerned in each case to artificially lower the tax paid in the respective country, not corresponding to respective market conditions. As a result, a large portion of the Starbucks' coffee roasting company profits is shifted abroad, and Fiat's financing company only paid taxes on underestimated profits. Moreover, on August 30, 2016 the Commission has concluded that Ireland granted undue tax benefits of up to EUR 13 billion to Apple (https://ec.europa.eu/commission/presscorner/detail/en/IP_16_2923).

54 Kristina Povazanova and Hana Kovacikova, Multinational tax avoidance vs. European Commission, *Bratislava Law Review*, 1, 2017.

55 Kyle Richard, Are all tax rulings state aid? Examining the European Commission recent state aid decisions, *Houston Business and Tax Law Journal*, XVIII, ISSN: 1543–2602.

well-represented in the sample of rulings chosen by the Commission for state aid analysis, providing some evidence that the Commission's investigations were, to some extent, triggered and informed by these prior events. The LuxLeaks scandal provides evidence of widespread Multinational Tax Avoidance. Shortly after the LuxLeaks scandal, the European Parliament and the European Commission began investigations into the tax regulatory practices and tax laws of the EU Member States that gave rise to the tax avoidance structures detailed in LuxLeaks.[56]

Although no specific definition of "harmful tax competition" is formulated in EU law, an area of state behavior (and in particular regulatory regimes adopted in national law) has been progressively identified that may be considered incompatible with the general principles set out in the Treaty.[57] However, it is just one of several European Commission decisions regarding the taxation of recently issued multinational transfer pricing activities, apparently in response to both the U.S. Senate inquiry into the tax practices of U.S. multinationals and the so-called "Luxembourg Leaks" or "LuxLeaks," documents published by the International Consortium of Investigative Journalists.[58]

The European Commission has initiated and finalized decisions adverse to Fiat, Starbucks, Apple, and Amazon based on specific transfer pricing methodologies used by those firms, and endorsed by tax authorities in Luxembourg, the Netherlands, and Ireland, arguing that each received illegal state aid. The Commission also found that the entire tax ruling practice in Belgium constituted illegal state aid. At present, the Commission Decisions which have been finalized are each under appeal.[59]

The scheme discovered in the EU targeted more than three hundred large multinational corporations – including Fiat – and has been in place since 2002. Large multinationals would have been offered very favorable tax treatment by national tax authorities on a case-by-case basis: the authorities issued mandatory written interpretations of the law in relation to the company in question (so-called advance tax rulings). It soon turned out that the practice of early tax rulings as an instrument of international tax

56 Kyle Richard, Are all tax rulings state aid? Examining the European Commission recent state aid decisions, *Houston Business and Tax Law Journal*, XVIII, ISSN: 1543–2602.

57 Pietro Boria, *Taxation in European Union*, 2nd ed., Cham, Switzerland, Springer International Publishing, 2017, ISBN 978-3-319-53918-8, ISBN 978-3-319-53919-5 (eBook), doi: 10.1007/978-3-319-53919-5, Library of Congress Control Number: 2017934921.

58 Kyle Richard, Are all tax rulings state aid? Examining the European Commission recent state aid decisions, *Houston Business and Tax Law Journal*, XVIII, ISSN: 1543–2602.

59 Kyle Richard, Are all tax rulings state aid? Examining the European Commission recent state aid decisions, *Houston Business and Tax Law Journal*, XVIII, ISSN: 1543–2602.

competition and the alleged tax avoidance for multinationals was by no means limited to Luxembourg: equal practices were used by Belgium, the Netherlands, and Ireland. The latter is the scene of the Apple case.[60]

The final European Commission Decisions have been issued based on the application of the arm's length principle contained in non-binding OECD guidance, without regard to whether the Member State has implemented the arm's length principle in its national tax legislation. It is the case of the Commission's Starbucks Decision, the Commission's Fiat Decision, the Commission's Apple Decision, the Commission Decision Regarding the Belgian Tax Ruling Practice and the Commission's Opening Decision Regarding Amazon. The affected parties have appealed each of the Commission Decisions discussed here to the CJEU, given the substantial amounts at stake in each case, regardless of the ruling in the administrative procedure; although the grounds for appeal in each case appear similar, based on the public versions of the appeals, each is analyzed separately.

However, given the summary nature of the public version of the appeal documents, the analysis of the parties' legal arguments is limited.[61] According to the European Commission's Decisions, the tax advisers of Fiat and Starbucks prepared and sent special tax decisions on behalf of their clients, which were granted by the tax authorities of Luxembourg and, respectively, the Netherlands. However, these tax decisions were considered illegal under European law because they constitute state aid and Fiat and Starbucks had to pay fines. State aid was conceived as a process of capital accumulation resulting from state authorization regimes based on interactions between public and private sector actors. Thus, an observable symbiosis between the tax authorities and the transnational companies allowed the latter to use the tax regulations in a manipulative way, while the former exercised poor or unjustified control. We observe the potential illegal (even criminal) role of tax advisers and other professionals rarely held accountable for their actions.[62]

"Harmful tax competition" is thus identified with the adoption of fiscal policies by a Member State which leads to a subversive tax order compared to most other states, as it introduces elements of tax facilitation or tax benefits, which determines the location of economic agents on the territory of the same state, including the allocation of resources and factors of production,

60 Thomas Jaeger, Tax concessions for multinationals: in or out of the reach of state aid law?, *Journal of European Competition Law & Practice*, 8(4), 2017.

61 Kyle Richard, Are all tax rulings state aid? Examining the European Commission recent state aid decisions, *Houston Business and Tax Law Journal*, XVIII, ISSN: 1543–2602.

62 Nubia Evertsson, State aid and taxation of transnational companies: a study of state-corporate crime, *Crit Crim*, 25, 507–522, 2017, doi: 10.1007/s10612-017-9375-6

to the detriment of the state of residence (and therefore with an ignorance of the "natural" development of the business).[63] In this context, each of the European Commission Decisions finds that a Member State granted state aid in contravention of the Treaty of the Functioning of the European Union (TFEU), Article 107(1). Although it is clear that the European Commission can examine Member State tax ruling practices for the type of discrimination or "selectivity" that would constitute an illegal grant of state aid in contravention of the TFEU, the recent Commission Decisions exceeded the scope of the Commission's authority by questioning generally applicable principles and provisions of Member State law without showing that the challenged measures were selective.[64]

The tax rates in the Eastern EU Member States are usually lower than those in the western EU Member States.[65] An exception is Ireland, with a corporate tax rate of 12.5%, but the corporate profits are taxed twice, while the profits of partnerships (and individual owners) are taxed only once. Most income tax systems address the double economic taxation of corporate profits at the level of shareholders. In line with this approach in EU law, the belief that tax competition between different Member States must be seen as a negative factor, potentially appropriate to change the functioning of the common market and to distort the effectiveness of the principle of free competition, has gradually emerged.[66] The European Commission's Decisions have been harshly criticized by multinational companies and regulators, but seem to reflect previous criticisms of non-governmental organizations (NGOs) of both multinational corporations and low-tax jurisdictions. It appears that the Commission's area of competence to examine Member States' tax laws and tax regulatory practices under the principles of state aid is likely to be decided by the Court of Justice of the European Union in the next few years.[67]

In-depth discussion of the tax laws of each Member State reveals the heterogeneity of the tax laws within the EU, which is essential for

63 Pietro Boria, *Taxation in European Union*, 2nd ed., Cham, Switzerland, Springer International Publishing, 2017, ISBN 978-3-319-53918-8, ISBN 978-3-319-53919-5 (eBook), doi: 10.1007/978-3-319-53919-5, Library of Congress Control Number: 2017934921.

64 Kyle Richard, Are all tax rulings state aid? Examining the European Commission recent state aid decisions, *Houston Business and Tax Law Journal*, XVIII, ISSN: 1543–2602.

65 Mihaela Tofan, *European financial law*, Iaşi, Romania, University Alexandru Ioan Cuza of Iasi Publishing House, 2019, ISBN 978-606-714-544-1

66 Pietro Boria, *Taxation in European Union*, 2nd ed., Cham, Switzerland, Springer International Publishing, 2017, ISBN 978-3-319-53918-8, ISBN 978-3-319-53919-5 (eBook), doi: 10.1007/978-3-319-53919-5, Library of Congress Control Number: 2017934921.

67 Kyle Richard, Are all tax rulings state aid? Examining the European Commission recent state aid decisions, *Houston Business and Tax Law Journal*, XVIII, ISSN: 1543–2602.

understanding the fundamental dispute between the Member States and the European Commission. This heterogeneity is the result of the EU's supranational and probably federalist system and has given rise to many tax minimization techniques used by US and EU multinational organizations. As a result of this structure, the European Union does not have a single, cohesive tax system. Member States are free to establish national tax law, and state aid can be found for any measure of the Member State that offers an advantage to one actor over others, and tax rulings have long been taken into account in this analysis. CJEU case-law provides for a four-prong approach to determining whether state aid exists.[68]

The General Court has issued its ruling in Cases T-760/15 and T-636/16, regarding the transfer pricing and the fiscal and procedural autonomy of the Member States on September 24, 2019, in the Fiat case,[69] in which the European Commission concluded that the methodology accepted by the Netherlands tax authorities for allocating the profits between the company subsidiaries was not in line with the arm's length principle and led to a reduction in a tax burden for Starbucks Manufacturing Emea BV, established in Amsterdam, Netherlands (par. 51). The fiscal authorities in Netherlands have conducted the advance price agreement indirectly awarding a state aid, which, in Commission opinion, should be annulled and the entire amount recovered to the state budget. After in-depth analysis of the factual context, presented evidence, and the regulation, the General Court concluded (par. 559–560) that the contested decision did not suffice to demonstrate that the advance price agreement had led to a tax advantage for the taxpayer in Netherland, so it should be annulled. The decision was not appealed by the Commission,[70] a possible explanation being the fact that the Commission may have lost in the Starbucks state aid case and won in the Fiat case, but it actually won both cases in principle. The General Court stated that the Commission has the power to review Member States' tax decisions on their compliance with a competition principle derived from EU law. The main difference between the two cases (i.e., the explanation why their result was not the same) was that, in the Starbucks case, the Commission did not show

68 Kyle Richard, Are all tax rulings state aid? Examining the European Commission recent state aid decisions, *Houston Business and Tax Law Journal*, XVIII, ISSN: 1543–2602.

69 The Judgment of the general Court (Seventh Chamber, Extended Composition) from September 24, 2019 in Cases T-760/15 and T-636/16 is available at: https://curia.europa.eu/juris/document/document.jsf?text=&docid=218101&pageIndex=0&doclang=en&mode=lst&dir=&occ=first&part=1&cid=96328, retrieved on December 20, 2021.

70 Dimitrios Kyriazis, *Why the EU Commission won't appeal the Starbucks judgment*, 2019, available at: https://mnetax.com/why-the-eu-commission-wont-appeal-the-starbucks-judgment-37043, retirieved on October 15, 2021.

that the Netherlands had departed from fair competition principle at the time of the tax ruling, therefore, no state aid advantage was found. On the other hand, the Commission's analysis in the Fiat case was more rigorous, which means that it could illustrate the granting of tax advantage by Luxembourg through the Fiat tax decision. In the Court's view, the other state aid conditions were also met, so that Luxembourg lost the case. In other words, in both the Starbucks and Fiat cases, the Commission won the important legal part, but in Starbucks it lost, that is, it failed to prove that Starbucks' tax judgment deviated from the fair competition principle.

In the Apple case, the annulment of the European Commission Decision C(2016) 5605 final of August 30, 2016 on state aid SA.38373 (2014/C) (ex 2014/NN) (ex 2014/CP) was implemented by Ireland, with support from the Grand Duchy of Luxembourg (intervener in Case T-778/16), Apple Sales International and Apple Operations Europe, both established in Cork – Ireland (applicants in Case T-892/16). After rejection of the USA intervention in Cases T-778/16 and T-892/16 (a solution which was confirmed by CJEU orders), the General Court had its judgment in the Seventh Chamber, Extended Composition, on July 15, 2020. The judgment is formulated on bases of state aid implemented by Ireland, which has been declared incompatible with the internal market and unlawful by the European Commission, considering previous tax decisions (tax rulings) and selective tax advantages, in the view of arm's length principle.[71] The judgment is thoroughly written, all the factual and the legal circumstances being exhausted. There are manifold explicit references to the OECD guidelines (par. 36, 91, 129, 167, 171–172, 196, 217, 219, 230–232, 235–237, 239–242, 244–245, 248–249, 252, 259, 316, 319, 321–325, 330, 335, 338–339, 357, 361, 363–364, 367–368, 372, 409–410, 446, 455, 472, 498) both in observing parties' arguments and in the reasoning of the judgment. The arguments used by the court refer to the lack of proof to sustain the view of the European Commission on the creation of jobs and the allocation of profit, using the comparable company, the arm's length principle in the view that the allocation of profits among several associated companies depends on the functions performed, the risks assumed, and the assets used by each company. Par. 498 of the judgment characterizes the objective analysis for the allocation of profits, that includes, first, identifying the activities performed by the branch, the assets it uses for its functions and the related risks that it assumes and,

71 The Judgment of the General Court (Seventh Chamber, Extended Composition) from July 15, 2020 (*) in Cases T-778/16 and T-892/16 is available at: https://curia.europa.eu/juris/document/document.jsf?text=&docid=228621&pageIndex=0&doclang=en&mode=lst&dir=&occ=first&part=1&cid=25840, retrieved on December 20, 2021.

second, determining the value of that type of activity on the market. Such an analysis corresponds, in essence, to the analysis proposed by the authorized OECD Approach. In its conclusions, the General Court held that the European Commission failed in showing that, by issuing the contested tax rulings, the Irish tax authorities had granted Apple Sales International and Apple Operations Europe a selective advantage for the purposes of Article 107(1) TFEU, so the contested decision was annulled. Currently, the case is under appeal at the CJEU (Commission v Ireland and Others Case C-465/20 P), the most recent order being issued on September 23, 2021, on the information treated as confidential at first instance.[72]

On May 12, 2021 the General Court held its judgment in Cases T-816/17 and T-318/18, responding to the applicants Grand Duchy of Luxembourg, Ireland, Amazon EU Sàrl, established in Luxembourg (Luxembourg) and Amazon.com, Inc., established in Seattle, Washington (United States) versus European Commission, ACTIONS pursuant to Article 263 TFEU for the annulment of Commission Decision (EU) 2018/859 of October 4, 2017 on state aid SA.38944 (2014/C) (ex 2014/NN) implemented by Luxembourg to Amazon (OJ 2018 L 153, p. 1).[73] The judgment specifically admitted (par. 112) that according to settled case-law, while direct taxation, as EU law currently stands, falls within the competence of the Member States, they must nonetheless exercise that competence consistently with EU law. Thus, intervention by the Member States in matters of direct taxation, even if it relates to issues that have not been harmonized in the European Union, is not excluded from the scope of the rules on the monitoring of state aid (see the previously mentioned judgment of September 24, 2019, Netherlands and Others v Commission, T-760/15 and T-636/16, EU:T:2019:669, paragraph 142). Accordingly, the Commission may classify a tax measure as state aid so long as the conditions for such a classification are satisfied. The court held the situation that when the public authorities grant certain undertakings favorable tax treatment which, although not involving a transfer of state resources, places the recipients in a more favorable financial situation than that of other taxpayers constitutes state aid for the purposes

72 The order of the President of the Court from September 23, 2021 Appeal – Intervention – Confidentiality – Information treated as confidential at first instance In Case C-465/20 P is available at: https://curia.europa.eu/juris/document/document.jsf?text=&docid=246927&pageIndex=0&doclang=en&mode=lst&dir=&occ=first&part=1&cid=63141, retrieved on January 20, 2021.

73 The Judgment of the General Court in Cases In Cases T-816/17 and T-318/18 from May 12, 2021 is available at: https://curia.europa.eu/juris/document/document.jsf?text=&docid=241188&pageIndex=0&doclang=en&mode=lst&dir=&occ=first&part=1&cid=112578, retrieved on October 15, 2021.

of Article 107(1) TFEU (par. 114). The position of the recipient as a result of the application of the measure at issue must be compared with his or her position in the absence of the measure at issue. In determining the fiscal position of an integrated company which is part of a group of undertakings, it must be noted at the outset that the pricing of intra-group transactions carried out by that company is not determined under market conditions. That pricing is agreed to by companies belonging to the same group, and is therefore not subject to market forces (par. 117). It should also be noted that when the Commission uses the arm's length principle to check whether the taxable profit of an integrated undertaking pursuant to a tax measure corresponds to a reliable approximation of a taxable profit generated under market conditions, the Commission can identify an advantage within the meaning of Article 107(1) TFEU only if the variation between the two comparables goes beyond the inaccuracies inherent in the methodology used to obtain that approximation (judgment of September 24, 2019, Netherlands and Others v Commission, T-760/15 and T-636/16, EU:T:2019:669, paragraph 152). The judgment proved that the Commission failed to prove the breach of the EU law, so the decision was annulled. The case is under appeal at the CJEU, Case C-815/21 P, and the reports of cases are not yet being published.

The European case-law in taxation includes relevant interpretation also in connection to Google company (i.e., Google Ireland), the freedom to provide services being recently addressed in Judgment of the Grand Chamber of the Court from March 3, 2020.[74] The Court observed the conformity of the Hungarian tax law to the European legal order, accepting the administrative liabilities for non-residence taxpayer, while forbidding a sanction for breaching the tax administrative liability represented by a fine with an unjustified mechanism of multiplication. The solution is under appeal at the CJEU (Case before the Court of Justice C-815/21 P) and the reports on cases are not available yet.

Recently, another case concerning Google has entered the appeal procedure at CJEU (C-48/22 P – Google and Alphabet v Commission, Google Shopping). Although not in direct connection with tax provision but with the dominant position restraints, the judgment of the General Court might generate effects also on the fiscal interpretation of the EU legal order.[75]

74 The Judgment of the Court (Grand Chamber) from March 3, 2020 in Case C-482/18 is available at: https://curia.europa.eu/juris/document/document.jsf?text=&docid=223981&pageIndex=0&doclang=EN&mode=lst&dir=&occ=first&part=1&cid=123189, retrieved on October 15, 2021.

75 The Judgment of the General Court (Ninth Chamber, Extended Composition) from the November 10, 2021 in Case T-612/17 is available at: https://curia.europa.eu/juris/

In par. 596 the Court held from the examination of the pleas concerning the finding of an infringement of Article 102 TFEU set out in Article 1 of the contested decision that that finding must be upheld to the extent that it concerns the abuse of a dominant position on the national markets for specialized product search services in the 13 countries referred to in that provision. However, that article must be annulled in so far only as it relates to the abuse of a dominant position on the national markets for general search services in those countries based on the existence of anticompetitive effects in those markets. Furthermore, in view of the fact that the Commission correctly concluded that Google had abused its dominant position on the national markets for specialized product search services, the action must be dismissed insofar as it also seeks annulment of the rest of the contested decision, ordering Google to bring to an end the infringement established in Article 1, ordering it to notify the Commission of the measures taken to that effect and providing for periodic penalty payments in the event of failure to comply with those obligations. Also, the amount of the fine imposed in the contested decision (par. 691 the basic amount is EUR 1,866,424,914) must be confirmed and consequently, the claim put forward in the alternative for annulment or reduction of the fine was rejected by the General Court (par. 704).

Some or even all the LuxLeaks cases may constitute illegal state aid. For example, Apple may be such a case. However, the presence of the aid must not be confused with the mere presence of a distortion of competition. Not all distortion practices are affected by the state aid ban. Fiat's decision fails to build a convincing argument in this regard, applies a crude and therefore overly inclusive standard and focuses on the wrong aspects of the case. Detecting and identifying discriminatory practices in early tax decisions seems to be the way to go in LuxLeaks cases to address relevant state aid measures, guess and suppress the national logic of corporate tax to inflate the aid law.[76] While analyzing the impact of the corporation taxation on the taxation of the individual income, three systems have to be considered:

1 Classical systems with full double taxation, when the corporate profits are taxed and the dividends are taxed one more time, at the moment when they are distributed; accordingly, in the classical system, the dividends are fully taxed twice.

---

document/document.jsf?text=&docid=250881&pageIndex=0&doclang=en&mode=lst&dir=&occ=first&part=1&cid=129291, retrieved on January 20, 2022.

76 Thomas Jaeger, Tax concessions for multinationals: in or out of the reach of state aid law?, *Journal of European Competition Law & Practice*, 8(4), 2017.

2 Double taxation avoidance systems, when taxes are not the liability of the company, nor the liability of the owners of the capital. The mechanism to ensure this special treatment may include the funding of the corporation taxes.
3 Double taxation mitigation systems, when the fiscal treatment includes taxes on both profits and shareholders' income from distributed dividends, but also some measure to diminish the payments or to reduce the impact on their assets for the shareholders. Within the EU, double taxation is avoided or mitigated at the shareholder level. Most Member States reduce either the number of taxable dividends or the tax rate which applies to dividends received by natural persons (shareholder relief).[77]

The use of national fiscal law measures offering tax benefits in favor of economic operators which are incorporated in that state is able to distort for the material point of view, the common framework of competition in business, determining obstacles and misfunctions in the normal activity of the internal market. In this context, the international actors which are involved in guarding the free competition in the market have constantly developed strategies to counteract the rules and practices permitted by particular Member States, when developing promotional goals on their territory.[78] Harmful tax competition is perceived as developing a source of divergence between Member States, because of its ability to impact national economic and fiscal policy decisions, which have to be antagonized by tight EU coordination.[79]

It was argued that the transfer restrictions affect the initial financing, as investors face the risk of losing the carry-over of accumulated losses in the corporation when introducing new ones or increasing the capital of existing investors.[80]

Harmful tax competition is identified as a major cause of the transfer of the tax burden from capital to labor by Member States. In fact, the provision of

77 Ulrich Schreiber, *International company taxation: an introduction to the legal and economic principles*, Berlin, Heidelberg, Springer-Verlag, 2013, ISBN 978-3-642-36305-4, doi: 10.1007/978-3-642-36306-1.

78 Pietro Boria, *Taxation in European Union*, 2nd ed., Cham, Switzerland, Springer International Publishing, 2017, ISBN 978-3-319-53918-8, ISBN 978-3-319-53919-5 (eBook), doi: 10.1007/978-3-319-53919-5, Library of Congress Control Number: 2017934921.

79 Pietro Boria, *Taxation in European Union*, 2nd ed., Cham, Switzerland, Springer International Publishing, 2017, ISBN 978-3-319-53918-8, ISBN 978-3-319-53919-5 (eBook), doi: 10.1007/978-3-319-53919-5, Library of Congress Control Number: 2017934921.

80 Anna Theresa Buhrle and Christoph Spengel, *Tax law and the transfer of start-up losses: a european overview and categorization*, Discussion Paper No. 19–037 | 09/, Berlin, Leibniz Association, ZEW, 2019.

preferential tax regimes is capable to attract mainly higher-income entrants (such as capital and businesses), but not the labor force, which is configured as a strong factor rooted in native and poorly mobilized territory.[81] Most European Member States use anti-trafficking rules, preventing the acquisition of simple corporate companies with large tax losses carried forward so that the tax asset can be used in profitable companies. However, other corporations may be unintentionally affected by anti-abuse regulations if there is a change in ownership or activity. Design and development of loss transfer restrictions in the EU28 over a period of 19 years (2000–2018) proves that, over time, regulations have become more permissive, giving start-ups more opportunities to keep their losses at bay and therefore reducing the risk for investors.[82]

4.3 Jurisprudential approach on European tax regulation integration

Nowadays and within the limits of the EU, a complex net has replaced the traditional pyramidal structure of the sources of law. The national legislative monism ratified in the nineteenth-century domestic codes is today undermined by different types of normative acts: directives, regulations, framework decisions, and community sources, on one hand, and international covenantal laws, on the other hand.[83] There is a deep modification not only in the framework of the traditional sources of law, but also an important challenge for the systems of law that mainly value the normative acts and not the jurisprudential input. The European continental systems of law underwent notable changes, accepting as a consequence of accessing the European integration project the guiding role of the former European Court of Justice (ECJ), today Court of Justice of the European Union (CJEU). The CJEU has the role of issuing the official interpretation of the European law and the mission to verify the validity of such an interpretation of the

81 Pietro Boria, *Taxation in European Union*, 2nd ed., Cham, Switzerland, Springer International Publishing, 2017, ISBN 978-3-319-53918-8, ISBN 978-3-319-53919-5 (eBook), doi: 10.1007/978-3-319-53919-5, Library of Congress Control Number: 2017934921.

82 Anna Theresa Buhrle and Christoph Spengel, *Tax law and the transfer of start-up losses: a european overview and categorization*, Discussion Paper No. 19–037 | 09/, Berlin, Leibniz Association, ZEW, 2019.

83 S. Lotito Fedele, The Ne Bis In idem principle in tax law: European and Italian frameworks, *Central European Public Administration Review*, 18(1), 51–68, 2020, available at: https://orcid.org/0000-0003-0108-9863

institutions, bodies, offices, or agencies of the Union.[84] As shown in the doctrine, the relationship between the national and supra-national judges has become important, given the powerful impact of the latter on the production and the practical impact of the domestic law.[85] The interaction of the national and European systems of law is even more complex when we assess the interpretation of the national law in view of the national constitutional court of the Member States. The fiscal case-law in particular has raised many questions about the impact and the interpretation of the supra-national law regarding the fundamental values of the Member States fundamental regulation, usually named constitution.[86] These situations bring into special attention aspects of international tax law, both at the domestic level and treaty law.

Nowadays, no tax expert in Europe may ignore the CJEU case-law in direct taxes, without losing the key to the solution of problems raised by cross-border situations. A complete analysis of relevant case-law for direct taxes situations is no longer a matter for a single publication, but for more extensive research, a challenge that concerns many scholars, doctrines being published in the various European languages. In the present EU legal order, the Member States are no longer free to exercise fully autonomously their

84 Article 267 (ex Article 234 TEC) of the Treaty on the Functioning of the European Union (consolidated version) part six: Institutional and financial provision – Title I: Institutional provisions, Chapter 1: The institutions, Section 5: The Court of Justice of the European Union – The Court of Justice of the European Union shall have jurisdiction to give preliminary rulings concerning:

1 the interpretation of the Treaties.
2 the validity and interpretation of acts of the institutions, bodies, offices or agencies of the Union.Where such a question is raised before any court or tribunal of a Member State, that court or tribunal may, if it considers that a decision on the question is necessary to enable it to give judgment, request the Court to give a ruling thereon.

Where any such question is raised in a case pending before a court or tribunal of a Member State against whose decisions there is no judicial remedy under national law, that court or tribunal shall bring the matter before the Court.

If such a question is raised in a case pending before a court or tribunal of a Member State with regard to a person in custody, the Court of Justice of the European Union shall act with the minimum of delay.

85 Karin Leijon, National courts and preliminary references: supporting legal integration, protecting national autonomy or balancing conflicting demands?, *West European Politics*, 2020, doi:10.1080/01402382.2020.1738113

86 S. Lotito Fedele, The Ne Bis In idem principle in tax law: European and Italian frameworks, *Central European Public Administration Review*, 18(1), 51–68, 2020, available at: https://orcid.org/0000-0003-0108-9863

taxing powers, but they must take into consideration the primacy of European law, both in respect to the formal law and the CJEU jurisprudence.[87] Further influence should be noted from soft law mechanisms, expanding the effect of the hard law taxation.

Synthetizing the CJEU in tax cases, we see that the cases were mainly designated to draw out the answer for these two questions:

1 Are the national tax practices discriminatory or not? In this case, the investigation targets the discrimination against cross-border activities compared to domestic ones.
2 Do the rules of the particular Member States create a limitation for the exercise of economic freedoms? In this case, both direct and indirect obstructive effects of the tax national rules are addressed.

The European legal order is observed and protected both:

- In the form of preceding control, when the national legislators (parliaments of the Member States) are obliged to carry out an intense evaluation in the course of legislative procedures, to establish the consistency of the domestic regulation with the European law
- In the form of subsequent control, carried out by the Court of Justice of the European Union, when it is properly invested

The CJEU is empowered to rule on claims in connection with the violation of the principle of subsidiarity by the EU legislative acts, which, according to the conditions laid down in Article 263 TFEU, are applied by Member States or transmitted by them in accordance with their legal order on behalf of their national Parliament or a chamber of the latter (Article 8 of the Protocol).[88]

As analyzed before in this work, taxation is one of the intrinsic components of state sovereignty, and the interaction of national tax systems remains a source of continuous disputes. The Union and Member States take measures to prevent the breaking of law and to simplify tax systems. At the same time, tax secrecy and deficiencies in solving the cases where the interaction of Member States' regulation is present, allow companies to exploit the differences in national tax systems. In addition, multinational companies use their presence in a large number of jurisdictions to

87 Pasquale Pistone, Towards European international tax law, *EC Tax Review*, 1, 2005.
88 Kyle Richard, Are all tax rulings state aid? Examining the European Commission recent state aid decisions, *Houston Business and Tax Law Journal*, XVIII, ISSN: 1543–2602.

benefit the complex corporate structures for the opportunities to exploit tax planning, which are not available for small businesses or individuals.[89] Analysis of the literature has shown that it is often necessary and justified that the Court of Justice of the European Union intervene, when the national courts ask for it or they have failed in interpreting the EU law. It is expected that the CJEU give consideration in elaboration of the ruling in the tax matters to the same fundamental values and ideas already expressed for other legal matters, stating the validity of specific transactions according to subjective elements (the purpose of obtaining a tax advantage contrary to the EU law), to be characterized based on a set of objective circumstances of the case. There are two situations when the CJEU is competent to take actions regarding regulation of Member States tax systems:

1 Using its legal reasoning and the interpretation of general principles of functioning of the European internal market and the subsequent effects of its judgments
2 Using limitation for the temporal effects for particular judgments

Indirectly, the literature shows there is a third possibility, namely the potential reduction of references for preliminary rulings sent by the Member States to the CJEU, a result of the efforts to protect the Member States budgets.[90]

The Court of Justice of the European Union has identified another important reason of general interest, from a conceptual point of view very close to the second mentioned here, namely the effectiveness of fiscal controls and audits. Initially, with regard to indirect taxation, the Court of Justice recognized the relevance of the grounds for safeguarding the effectiveness of fiscal supervision as a cause of justification in relation to the EU legal framework (see in particular Case 20.2.1979, C-120/78 Cassis de Dijon).[91]

It was not until the European judges decided the Schumacker case that Member States were required to exercise their taxing powers on cross-border situations in a way that respects the primacy of Community law (par. 29 *tax benefits granted only to residents of a Member State may constitute*

89 Kyle Richard, Are all tax rulings state aid? Examining the European Commission recent state aid decisions, *Houston Business and Tax Law Journal*, XVIII, ISSN: 1543–2602.

90 Katerina Pantazatou, Economic and political considerations of the court's case law post crisis: an exemple from tax law and the internal market, *CYELP*, 9, 77–118, 2013.

91 Pietro Boria, *Taxation in European Union*, 2nd ed., Cham, Switzerland, Springer International Publishing, 2017, ISBN 978-3-319-53918-8, ISBN 978-3-319-53919-5 (eBook), doi: 10.1007/978-3-319-53919-5, Library of Congress Control Number: 2017934921.

indirect discrimination by reason of nationality).[92] When the Saint-Gobain case was decided (Judgment of the Court from September 21, 1999),[93] tax treaties came in open conflict with Community law. The Court ruled in par. 39 that for those companies to which they are granted, the tax concessions represented by corporation tax relief for international groups and by indirect credit result in a lighter tax burden, so that the permanent establishments of companies having their corporate seat in another Member State ('non-resident companies') which cannot qualify for them are in a less favorable situation than resident companies, including German subsidiaries of non-resident companies. The refusal to grant the tax concessions in question to the permanent establishments in Germany of non-resident companies makes it less attractive for those companies to have intercorporate holdings through German branches, since under German law and double-taxation treaties the tax concessions in question can only be granted to German subsidiaries which, as legal persons, are subject to unlimited tax liability, which thus restricts the freedom to choose the most appropriate legal form for the pursuit of activities in another Member State, which the second sentence of the first paragraph of Article 52 of the Treaty expressly confers on economic operators (par. 43). Taxation of income and profits falls within the competence of the Member States, which are therefore at liberty to conclude bilateral double-taxation treaties with non-member countries. In the absence of community harmonization in this area, the question whether, in the case of dividends, the tax exemption for international groups should be granted to permanent establishments under a tax treaty concluded with a non-member country is not governed by community law (par. 55). In the case of a double-taxation treaty concluded between a Member State and a non-member country, the national treatment principle requires the Member State which is party to the treaty to grant to permanent establishments of non-resident companies the advantages provided for by that treaty on the same conditions as those which apply to resident companies (par. 59).

Therefore, negative integration has so far been the engine of the development of European International Tax Law.[94]

The rulings of European courts in tax matters and connected case-law evolved accordingly to the status of European integration, ensuring in fiscal litigations the proper applicability of the EU law's general principles

92 The Judgment of the Court from February 14, 1995 in Case C-279/93, available at: https://curia.europa.eu/juris/showPdf.jsf?text=&docid=99137&pageIndex=0&doclang=EN&mode=lst&dir=&occ=first&part=1&cid=947824, retrieved on January 20, 2022.

93 The Judgment of the Court from the September 21, 1999 in Case C-307/97 is available at: https://curia.europa.eu/juris/showPdf.jsf?text=&docid=44717&pageIndex=0&doclang=en&mode=lst&dir=&occ=first&part=1&cid=950148, retrieved on January 20, 2022.

94 Pasquale Pistone, Towards European international tax law, *EC Tax Review*, 1, 2005.

of subsidiarity and proportionality, simultaneously referring to particular aspects of the tax regulation such as the abuse of right in fiscal conduct (i.e., Case C-371/07,[95] Case C-101/16,[96] and, recently, Case C-664/21[97]), non-discriminatory treatment for the taxpayers (i.e., Case C-132/06[98] and, recently, in Case C-220/19[99]) and possible limitation of rights in national

95 Opinion of Advocate General Sharpston delivered on October 23, 2008 in Case C-371/07, Danfoss and AstraZeneca v Skatteministeriet Vestre Landsret – Denmark. Reference for a preliminary ruling concerning Sixth VAT Directive – Article 6(2) – Supplies of services carried out free of charge by a taxable person for purposes other than those of his business – Right to deduct VAT – Second subparagraph of Article 17(6) – Member States' option to retain exclusions from the right to deduct which were provided for under their national laws when the Sixth Directive came into force, available at: https://curia.europa.eu/juris/document/document.jsf?text=abuse%2Bof%2Bright&docid=66964&pageIndex=0&doclang=en&mode=req&dir=&occ=first&part=1&cid=3796549#ctx1, retrieved on December 20, 2021.

96 Judgment of the Court (Second Chamber) from October 19, 2017 in Case C-101/16, SC Paper Consult SRL v Direcţia Regională a Finanţelor Publice Cluj-Napoca, Romania. Reference for a preliminary ruling regarding Taxation – Value added tax (VAT) – Directive 2006/112/EC – Right to deduct – Conditions governing the exercise of that right – Article 273 – National measures – Fight against tax evasion and tax avoidance – Invoice issued by a taxpayer declared 'inactive' by the tax authorities – Risk of tax evasion – Refusal of the right to deduct – Proportionality – Refusal to take into account evidence of the absence of tax evasion or tax losses – Limitation of the temporal effects of the judgment to be delivered, available at: https://curia.europa.eu/juris/document/document.jsf?text=abuse%2Bof%2Bright&docid=195735&pageIndex=0&doclang=EN&mode=req&dir=&occ=first&part=1&cid=3799417#ctx1, retrieved on December 20, 2021.

97 Request for a preliminary ruling in Case C-664/21 from October 13, 2021, NEC PLUS ULTRA COSMETICS AG v. Republic of Slovenia, available at: https://curia.europa.eu/juris/showPdf.jsf?text=&docid=251802&pageIndex=0&doclang=en&mode=lst&dir=&occ=first&part=1&cid=3801724, retrieved on January 20, 2022.

98 Judgment of the Court (Grand Chamber) from July 17, 2008 in Case C-132/06, Commission of the European Communities v. Italian Republic, concerning the failure of a Member State to fulfil obligations – Article 10 EC – Sixth VAT Directive – Obligations under domestic rules – Control of taxable transactions – Amnesty, available at: https://curia.europa.eu/juris/document/document.jsf?text=non-discriminatory%2Btreatment%2Bfor%2Bthe%2Btaxpayers&docid=67785&pageIndex=0&doclang=en&mode=req&dir=&occ=first&part=1&cid=3802820#ctx1, retrieved on October 15, 2021.

99 Judgment of the court (Tenth Chamber) form March 3, 2021 in Case C-220/19, Promociones Oliva Park SL v. Tribunal Económico Administrativo Regional (TEAR) de la Comunidad Valenciana, Request for a preliminary ruling under Article 267 TFEU – Directive 2008/118/EC – General arrangements for excise duty – Article 1(2) – Other indirect taxes on excise goods – Directive 2009/28/EC – Promotion of the use of energy from renewable sources – Article 1 and Article 3(1), (2) and (3)(a), the latter paragraph read in conjunction with Article 2(k) – Directive 2009/72/EC – Common rules for the internal market in electricity – Tax on the value of electricity production – Nature and structure of the tax – Electricity from renewable sources and electricity from non-renewable sources taxed in the same way, available at: https://curia.europa.eu/juris/document/document.jsf?text=non-discriminatory%2Btreatment%2Bfor%2Bthe%2Btaxpayers&docid=238442&pageIndex=0&doclang=EN&mode=req&dir=&occ=first&part=1&cid=3802820#ctx1, retrieved on October 15, 2021.

legislations (Case C-97/09,[100] Case C-480/16,[101] and, recently, joined Cases C-115/16, C-118/16, C-119/16, and C-299/16[102]).

The gap between the provisions of the EU law and national tax systems, in particular the limit of the principles of non-discrimination and non-restriction, reflects the possibility or the risk of international tax evasion (or tax avoidance).[103] The concept of tax avoidance and the application of the "abuse of rights" doctrine in this context have been discussed in many jurisdictions for the last two decades. The practical part of this debate is devoted to establishing the demarcation line for illegal conduct (tax evasion) toward potential abusive actions (which form tax avoidance) and acceptable behavior (tax planning). From an academic point of view, most writings concern

100 Judgment of the Court (Grand Chamber) from October 26, 2010 in Case C-97/09, Ingrid Schmelz v. Finanzamt Waldviertel, Austria. Reference for a preliminary ruling under Article 234 EC and Sixth VAT Directive – Articles 24(3) and 28i – Directive 2006/112/EC – Article 283(1)(c) – Validity – Articles 12 EC, 43 EC and 49 EC – Principle of equal treatment – Special scheme for small undertakings – Exemption from VAT – Benefit of the exemption refused to taxable persons established in other Member States – Definition of 'annual turnover', available at: https://curia.europa.eu/juris/document/document.jsf?text=non-residents%2Brights%2B&docid=78735&pageIndex=0&doclang=EN&mode=req&dir=&occ=first&part=1&cid=3806305#ctx1, retrieved on October 15, 2021.

101 Judgment of the Court (Fifth Chamber) from June 21, 2018 in Case C-480/16, Fidelity v Skatteministeret, Denmark. Request for a preliminary ruling under Article 267 TFEU – Free movement of capital and liberalisation of payments – Restrictions – Taxation of dividends paid to undertakings for collective investment in transferable securities (UCITS) – Dividends paid by companies resident in one Member State to non-resident UCITS – Tax exemption for dividends paid by companies resident in one Member State to resident UCITS – Justifications – Balanced allocation between Member States of the power to impose taxes – Coherence of the tax system – Proportionality, available at: https://curia.europa.eu/juris/document/document.jsf?text=non-residents%2Brights%2B&docid=203226&pageIndex=0&doclang=EN&mode=req&dir=&occ=first&part=1&cid=3806305#ctx1, retrieved on October 15, 2021.

102 Judgment of the Court (Grand Chamber) from February 26, 2019 in Joined Cases C-115/16, C-118/16, C-119/16 and C-299/16. Reference for a preliminary ruling – Approximation of laws – Common system of taxation applicable to interest and royalty payments made between associated companies of different Member States – Directive 2003/49/EC – Beneficial owner of the interest and royalties – Article 5 – Abuse of rights – Company established in a Member State and paying to an associated company established in another Member State interest all or almost all of which is then transferred outside the European Union – Subsidiary subject to an obligation to withhold tax on the interest at source, available at: https://curia.europa.eu/juris/document/document.jsf?text=non-residents%2Brights%2B&docid=211053&pageIndex=0&doclang=EN&mode=req&dir=&occ=first&part=1&cid=3806305#ctx1, retrieved on October 15, 2021.

103 Pietro Boria, *Taxation in European Union*, 2nd ed., Cham, Switzerland, Springer International Publishing, 2017, ISBN 978-3-319-53918-8, ISBN 978-3-319-53919-5 (eBook), doi: 10.1007/978-3-319-53919-5, Library of Congress Control Number: 2017934921.

the legal requirements for the application of a doctrine on abuse of rights. While some stress the effectiveness of purposive construction in the fight against tax avoidance, others acknowledge some value-added in a statutory general anti-avoidance rule.[104]

Without considering this assumption more than a partial result of our investigation, it is obvious that the EU legal system allows the national taxation system to determine the taxpayers' actions targeting tax avoidance or tax evasion, simultaneously establishing some limitations to Member States' ruling competence, with regards to the prohibition of restrictions for the fundamental freedoms of European law. As literature has mentioned,[105] the CJEU warns about the risk of using the reason of national interest in an indiscriminate manner, which constitutes a possible way to benefit from the EU legal order in favor of the protectionist and self-oriented goals of the Member States.

In the field of European secondary law, the application of anti-abuse concepts depends on the range of taxpayers' choices, which are allowed within the limits of the relevant provisions of directives in the tax sector. The Court does fully accept the existence of tax planning and the fact that the taxpayers may choose to structure their business, in order to reduce their tax liability (Case C-255/02 Halifax).[106] The illegal conduct exists when the tax planning is abusive, particularly when two conditions are met:

1 Without prejudice to the formal application of the conditions laid down in the relevant legal provisions, the transactions lead to the accumulation of a tax advantage the granting of which would be contrary to the purpose of the legal provisions.
2 It must be clear from a number of objective factors that the essential purpose of transactions is to obtain a tax advantage. Accordingly, the motivation in the Halifax Case (par. no. 75) specifically says there is no abuse if the economic activity carried out can have another explanation, besides the simple realization of the fiscal advantage.[107]

104 Wolfgang Schoen, *Abuse of rights and European tax law*, available at: www.cambridge.org/core, retrieved on July 23, 2020.

105 Pietro Boria, *Taxation in European Union*, 2nd ed., Cham, Switzerland, Springer International Publishing, 2017, ISBN 978-3-319-53918-8, ISBN 978-3-319-53919-5 (eBook), doi: 10.1007/978-3-319-53919-5, Library of Congress Control Number: 2017934921.

106 Wolfgang Schoen, *Abuse of rights and European tax law,* available at: www.cambridge.org/core, retrieved on July 23, 2020.

107 Frans Vanistendael, Halifax and Cadbury Schweppes: one single European theory of abuse in tax law?, *EC Tax Review*, 4, 2006.

In a successive line of case-law, the court accepted that restrictive anti-avoidance measures may exceptionally be justified, if they are particularly addressing the entirely artificial constructions, without economic substance, which seek to avoid the tax burden that would otherwise apply.[108] In the Halifax decision, the CJEU has clarified substantially the role and the concept of abusive practices in the area of VAT. However there remains one cloud of ambiguity[109] regarding the distinction between the sole purpose (also addressed in Case C-4/20[110] and, even more recently, in Case C-607/20[111]) and the essential purpose (Case C-26/18,[112] and, recently, in Case C-513/20[113]).

108 See http://curia.europa.eu/en/content/juris/index.htm for Case C-231/05 (Oy AA), Case C-196/04 (Cadbury Schweppes plc v. Commissioners of Inland Revenue); Case C-446/03 (Marks & Spencer plc v. Halsey).

109 Frans Vanistendael, Halifax and Cadbury Schweppes: one single European theory of abuse in tax law?, *EC Tax Review*, 4, 2006.

110 Judgment of the Court (First Chamber) from May 20, 2021 in Case C-4/20, 'ALTI' OOD v Direktor na Direktsia 'Obzhalvane i danachno-osiguritelna praktika' Plovdiv pri Tsentralno upravlenie na Natsionalnata agentsia za prihodite, Bulgaria. Reference for a preliminary ruling regarding Common system of value added tax (VAT) – Directive 2006/112/EC – Article 205 – Persons liable for payment of VAT to the public exchequer – Joint and several liability of the recipient of a taxable supply which has exercised its right to deduct VAT knowing that the person liable for payment of that tax would not pay it – Obligation of such a recipient to pay the VAT not paid by the person liable for payment and the default interest due on account of that person's failure to pay the VAT, available at: https://curia.europa.eu/juris/document/document.jsf?text=sole%2Bpurpose%2B&docid=241467&pageIndex=0&doclang=EN&mode=req&dir=&occ=first&part=1&cid=3822911#ctx1, retrieved on October 15, 2021.

111 Opinion of Advocate General ĆAPETA, delivered on January 27, 2022 in Case C-607/20, GE Aircraft Engine Services Ltd v. The Commissioners for Her Majesty's Revenue & Customs. Request for a preliminary ruling regarding Value added tax – Transfers of vouchers as taxable transactions – Article 26(1)(b) of the VAT Directive – Concept of 'private use or that of his staff or, more generally, for purposes other than those of his business' – Provision of vouchers, free of charge, to staff as part of an employee reward scheme, available at: https://curia.europa.eu/juris/document/document.jsf?text=sole%2Bpurpose%2B&docid=252845&pageIndex=0&doclang=EN&mode=req&dir=&occ=first&part=1&cid=3812811#ctx1, retrieved on January 30, 2022.

112 Judgment of the Court (First Chamber) from July 10, 2019 in Case C-26/18, Federal Express Corporation Deutsche Niederlassung v. Hauptzollamt Frankfurt am Main, Germany, Reference for a preliminary ruling – Customs Union – Regulation (EEC) No 2913/92 – Articles 202 and 203 – Customs duties on imports – Incurrence of a customs debt on account of infringements of customs legislation – Taxation – Value added tax (VAT) – Directive 2006/112/EC – Article 2(1)(d) and Article 30 – VAT on importation – Chargeable event – Concept of 'importation' of goods – Requirement that the goods must enter the economic network of the Union – Carriage of those goods to a Member State other than that in which the customs debt was incurred, available at: https://curia.europa.eu/juris/document/document.jsf?text=essential%2Bpurpose%2B&docid=216044&pageIndex=0&doclang=EN&mode=req&dir=&occ=first&part=1&cid=3825608#ctx1, accessed on October 15, 2021.

113 Judgment of the Court (Seventh Chamber) from January 13, 2022 in Case C-513/20, Autoridade Tributária e Aduaneira Portugal v. Termas Sulfurosas de Alcafache SA,

In the Cadbury Schweppes case, there were three main questions:

- Firstly, whether establishing a company in another Member State of the EU, solely to take advantage of a more favorable tax regime than in the home state constitutes an abuse of the freedoms of establishment, and the CJEU expressly stated in paragraph 37 of the ruling that the purpose of benefiting from more favorable legislation in another Member State does not in itself constitute an abuse of the freedom of establishment.
- Secondly, whether the way the British CFC rules are formulated incorporates a restriction in the exercise of the right of establishment or a discrimination, when Cadbury Schweppes was exercising this right in a genuine manner and European court firmly holds in paragraph 49 of the ruling that the advantage resulting from the establishment of a subsidiary in a low tax jurisdiction, other than the one in which the parent company has been incorporated, cannot by itself authorize that Member State to offset that advantage by less favorable tax treatment of the parent company. As a result, it is obvious that diminishing tax revenue is not in itself an indicator of overriding public interest and it is not justificative for any restriction or discrimination in the right of establishment in the European internal market.
- Thirdly, the questions if the British CFC legislation would be viewed as constituting a prohibited restriction or discrimination, whether it could be justified on grounds of prevention of tax avoidance and if it was proportionate in relation to its goal were answered by the European court in paragraph 51 of the ruling, by resuming that a national regulation restricting the freedom of establishment may be justified when it specifically targets the completely artificial arrangements aimed at eluding the application of the Member State's concerned legal framework.[114]

The questions of abuse in Cadbury Schweppes were raised in quite a different way from Halifax. The court explained that an agreement is completely artificial if it does not imply the goals of a real economic activity, such as "letter box" companies that are considered to lack economic substance

---

Reference for a preliminary ruling – Common system of value added tax (VAT) – Directive 2006/112/EC – Article 132(1)(b) – Exemptions for certain activities in the public interest – Exemption of hospital and medical care – Closely related activities – Thermal treatment – Amount charged for compiling an individual file including the user's clinical history, available at: https://curia.europa.eu/juris/document/document.jsf?text=essential%2Bpurpose%2B&docid=252132&pageIndex=0&doclang=EN&mode=req&dir=&occ=first&part=1&cid=3825608#ctx1, accessed on January 30, 2022.

114 Frans Vanistendael, Halifax and Cadbury Schweppes: one single European theory of abuse in tax law?, *EC Tax Review*, 4, 2006.

(Cadbury Schweppes, 2006).[115] The question was not one of artificial construction within the tax system of a particular Member State, but rather a straightforward construction to take advantage of tax benefits provided in the national legislation of another Member State. Whether the establishment in the other Member State was genuine and effective and whether the home state was entitled to defend itself by imposing Controlled Foreign Corporation (CFC) legislation were also debated.[116]

Against this background, Advocate-Generals Geelhoed, Leger, and Mengozzi have pointed out[117] that Member States are not able to act solely against "harmful tax competition." If this is true, the simple fact that the taxpayer decides to move his/her business from a high-tax state to a low-tax state does not mandatorily demand for the application of anti-abuse provisions in the Member State which is deprived of its legitimate tax revenue, even if the tax benefits offered by the other Member State can objectively be qualified as elements of harmful tax competition. The conclusion is that CJEU used in its decisions the argument of the economic reality of the transaction to infirm tax avoidance. In the Halifax case the economic reality of domestic VAT transactions is the major reason for the final ruling, while in Cadbury Schweppes the economic reality is the exercise of the fundamental freedom to use cross-border transactions within the European internal market. The form in which the economic reality of the transaction is explained in the reasoning of the court presents differences only with regards to the viewpoint of the two case-laws, not in substance.

A more interesting difference between the Halifax and Cadbury cases is in the possibility of the national courts in VAT to decide whether the tax motive is "essential" compared to some other non-tax explanations, while the cross-border economic reality of the transactions determines the refutation of tax avoidance and the purpose of targeting the tax advantage has no effect (recently addressed in Case C-220/19[118]). When the CJEU, as it

115 Servaas Van Thiel, The direct income tax case law of the European court of justice: past, trends and future developments, *Tax Law Review*, 62, 2008, ISSN: 0040–0041, Author/Editor: New York University School of Law, Publisher: Warren, Gorham & Lamont Series: Current periodical series, Language: English, Country of publication: United States of America.

116 Frans Vanistendael, Halifax and Cadbury Schweppes: one single European theory of abuse in tax law?, *EC Tax Review*, 4, 2006.

117 Wolfgang Schoen, *Abuse of rights and European tax law,* available at: www.cambridge.org/core, retrieved on July 23, 2020.

118 Judgment of the Court (Tenth Chamber) from March 3, 2021 in Case C-220/19, Promociones Oliva Park SL v. Tribunal Económico Administrativo Regional (TEAR) de la Comunidad Valenciana, Spain. Reference for a preliminary ruling – Directive 2008/118/EC – General arrangements for excise duty – Article 1(2) – Other indirect taxes on

should, had to decide that the effective economic existence of the transactions would preclude the application of anti-avoidance provisions, it would in fact use only one single rule: if there were an effective economic transaction on the basis of objective criteria which third parties can ascertain, the tax motive becomes irrelevant, even if it is significantly more important than the economic content of the transactions. Such a rule would also come very close to existing general anti-avoidance doctrine applicable in many Member States.[119]

It is observed in the relevant doctrine[120] that the cause of reasoning was found by the CJEU in the general scope to prevent tax avoidance, regarded as a subject which must weaken the effectiveness of the tax systems of Member States. In particular, most of the issues brought before the CJEU relate to cases of allocation of tax losses or tax benefits to the parent company within a group of companies established in different Member States, in order to allow taxable profits to be moved from the place of effective operations to another Member State which exercised lighter fiscal pressure on the economy, using lower taxes (Case 12/13/2005, C-446/2003 Marks & Spencer; Case 07/18/2007, C-231/2005 OY AA). It is reasonable to consider that this movement arrangement is not presumably artificial, if the operation reflects economic reality, such as in the case of the activity of CFC, when the companies physically exist in the host state, in terms of premises, staff, and equipment, while the activity is taking place in other Member States. Accordingly, the subsidiarity principle determines the competence of the national courts to decide whether the evidence for a certain operation is wholly artificial and without economic substance.

The national court is to decide if the domestic anti-avoidance measures are mainly intended to address artificial construction or whether their scope is too wide. National courts must present their decision after thorough analysis of every case-law presented to them, observing the general principle

excise goods – Directive 2009/28/EC – Promotion of the use of energy from renewable sources – Article 1 and Article 3(1), (2) and (3)(a), the latter paragraph read in conjunction with Article 2(k) – Directive 2009/72/EC – Common rules for the internal market in electricity – Tax on the value of electricity production – Nature and structure of the tax – Electricity from renewable sources and electricity from non-renewable sources taxed in the same way, available at: https://curia.europa.eu/juris/document/document.jsf?text=tax%2Badvantage%2Bno%2Beffect&docid=238442&pageIndex=0&doclang=EN&mode=req&dir=&occ=first&part=1&cid=3833622#ctx1, retrieved on October 15, 2021.

119 Frans Vanistendael, Halifax and Cadbury Schweppes: one single European theory of abuse in tax law?, *EC Tax Review*, 4, 2006.

120 Pietro Boria, *Taxation in European Union*, 2nd ed., Cham, Switzerland, Springer International Publishing, 2017, ISBN 978-3-319-53918-8, ISBN 978-3-319-53919-5 (eBook), doi: 10.1007/978-3-319-53919-5, Library of Congress Control Number: 2017934921.

of proportionality and strictly applying specific national or regional arguments, in respect to the due process requirements.

From the case-law of direct tax regulation, it is clear that European legislation does not provide for a discharge, or an exception of sovereignty or any other special status for income tax. Consequently, the way in which both the home Member State and the host Member State tax cross-border income is collected by EU subjects should be "constitutionally sound" in the two/many involved countries and the direct tax regulations are to be checked for consistency with the EU law, in general, and the rights deriving from the rule of internal market and non-discrimination, in particular.[121] So, the national courts are the ones to decide whether transactions are abusive, looking into the specifics of the operation, seeking the real substance and significance of the transactions concerned. In this respect, the national judge may take into account the purely artificial nature of the transaction and the legal, economic and/or personal links between the operators involved in the tax reduction scheme.[122]

The CJEU also stated that the identification of the tax advantage, as an "essential purpose" of operations, is not able to stand alone for the general condition of the recognition of abuse, but it identifies a minimum threshold of unacceptability of abuse of rights (Case 02/21/2008, C-425/06 Part Service).[123] Paragraph 56 of the Saint Gobain decision (C-307/97) could be the starting point in affirming the primacy of European law over that of the Member States in the taxation field, even in the presence of double taxation conventions, while the European court reassured that the Member States are empowered to establish the rules for taxation of income and wealth, aiming at eliminating and allocating competence of taxation for each one of them.[124]

Considering the taxpayer's autonomous right to decide the way of managing the business, limiting any kind of payment obligation (including the fiscal one), the feature of any abusive conduct should be analyzed in

121 Servaas Van Thiel, The direct income tax case law of the European court of justice: past, trends and future developments, *Tax Law Review*, 62, 2008, ISSN: 0040–0041, Author/Editor: New York University School of Law, Publisher: Warren, Gorham & Lamont Series: Current periodical series, Language: English, Country of publication: United States of America.

122 Frans Vanistendael, Halifax and Cadbury Schweppes: one single European theory of abuse in tax law?, *EC Tax Review*, 4, 2006.

123 Pietro Boria, *Taxation in European Union*, 2nd ed., Cham, Switzerland, Springer International Publishing, 2017, ISBN 978-3-319-53918-8, ISBN 978-3-319-53919-5 (eBook), doi: 10.1007/978-3-319-53919-5, Library of Congress Control Number: 2017934921.

124 Mario Tenore, The transfer of assets from a permanent establishment to its general enterprise in the light of European tax law, *International Tax Review Intertax*, 34(8–9), 2006.

connection with the specificity of the operating market. In line with this diagnosis approach, operations that are solely presented could be parts of the same unitary transaction, when the particular context reveals persuasively and forcibly that they all form together the same economic operation, so the tax treatment of the various segments of the operation are not to be analyzed separated, but within the principal operation (Case 02/21/2008, C-425/06 Part Service). Nevertheless, the evaluation of the taxpayer motivation and the reality of the economic purpose should be different for each case, taking into consideration the particular features (Case 09/12/2006, C-196/04, Cadbury Schweppes).[125]

Despite the fact that references to the prohibition of abusive tax transactions are present in particular rules dedicated to combating the fraudulent actions of taxpayers, with the specific intention to respect the application of EU regulations (see art. 11, no. 1, letter A of Directive n. 90/434/EEC; art. 1, par. 2, Directive n. 90/435/EEC; art. 5, Directive n. 2003/49/ EC), the CJEU has only recently defined the notion of abuse of law.[126] At the beginning, the Court has described the autonomous concept of abuse of tax law in connection to the regulation of value added tax (VAT), deciding that the taxpayer is not allowed to deduct the VAT paid on inputs if "transactions from which derive that right constitute an abusive practice" (Case 02/21/2006, C-255/02 Halifax). When the CJEU references were made to direct taxation, the reasoning stated that the freedom of establishment of the company cannot be restricted as the effect of a specific domestic tax measure, "unless it relates only to wholly artificial arrangements intended to escape the normally payable national tax" (Case 09/12/2006, C-196/04, Cadbury Schweppes). Both the Halifax and Cadbury decisions of the CJEU mentioned that the analyzed transactions developed by natural and/or legal persons resident in the European Union, which are built in a manner that was not directly required or implied by the economic activity (artificially constructed), proving diligence to the final goal of "obtaining a tax benefit" in contrast with the purposes pursued by the Treaty. If this hypothesis was valid, the conduct of the parties must be characterized as a typical kind of abuse of law.[127]

125 Pietro Boria, *Taxation in European Union*, 2nd ed., Cham, Switzerland, Springer International Publishing, 2017, ISBN 978-3-319-53918-8, ISBN 978-3-319-53919-5 (eBook), doi: 10.1007/978-3-319-53919-5, Library of Congress Control Number: 2017934921.

126 European Commission, *Guide to the case law of the European Court of Justice on Articles 56 et seq. TFEU – Freedom to provide services*, available at: http://ec.europa.eu/docsroom/translations/renditions/pdf, retrieved on May 12, 2020.

127 Pietro Boria, *Taxation in European Union*, 2nd ed., Cham, Switzerland, Springer International Publishing, 2017, ISBN 978-3-319-53918-8, ISBN 978-3-319-53919-5 (eBook), doi: 10.1007/978-3-319-53919-5, Library of Congress Control Number: 2017934921.

The CJEU has a special role to play in applying the principle of proportionality to the provisions of tax law. When considering the proportionality of a particular measure in this field, it has to establish specific indicators and proportion criteria. According to Article 5 of the Protocol on the application of subsidiarity and proportionality, the principles of reasoning lead to the conclusion that the objective of the EU can be better achieved at the latter level; it should be based on quality and, whenever possible, quantitative indicators.[128] The principle of proportionality consists of three sub-principles: suitability, necessity, and proportionality in the narrow sense.[129] All these sub-principles express the concept of efficiency, mandatory when applying the principle of proportionality to the constitutional rules and it is important to use them as imperative requirements. As a direct consequence, the European concept of principle is often used instead of the term "law." When there is a suspicion that the national tax law touches the fundamental freedom of the European internal market, it is mandatory to conduct a proportionality investigation, while two test questions are to be formulated:

- If respecting the particular national rule of law is able to conduct to the achievement of the specific objective established when the regulation came into force, in other words if the rule is able to lead to the intended goals (suitability test)
- If the particular national rule of law is too demanding for the achievement of the specific objective, established when the regulation came into force, in other words if the rule is too severe for leading to the intended goals (the necessity test)[130]

The suitability test did not generate major dispute in tax literature, while the necessity test did bring on the floor of academic discussions some controversies, especially in cases where the CJEU action was under suspicion of political decisions.[131] Terra and Wattel formulated serious critics when performing

128 Kyle Richard, Are all tax rulings state aid? Examining the European Commission recent state aid decisions, *Houston Business and Tax Law Journal*, XVIII, ISSN: 1543–2602.

129 Robert Alexy, Constitutional rights and proportionality, *Journal for Constitutional Theory and Philosophy of Law*, 22, 2014, available at: http://journals.openedition.org/revus/2783; doi: 10.4000/revus.2783; doi:10.4000/revus.2783.

130 Sjoerd Douma, *Optimization of tax sovereignty and free movement*, IBFD Doctoral Series, No. 21, Amsterdam, IBFD Publications BV, October 6, 2011, available at: https://ssrn.com/abstract=2997412

131 J. Ghosh, Tax law and the internal market: a critique of the principle of mutual recognition. *Cambridge Yearbook of European Legal Studies*, 16, 189–221, 2014, doi:10.1017/S1528887000002597

the necessity test.[132] As shown in our analysis in the previous sections of this publication, there is a continuous strain in tax law doctrine to reconcile the right of the Member States of the EU to determine their particular tax system and to protect tax sovereignty and, at the same time, to stop them from ruling tax regulation on cross-border transactions with impact to the EU law, i.e., designing less favorable conditions for extraterritorial activity in comparison to the whole national situation. The ideal conduct for every Member State is to keep the balance of the European law's fundamental freedoms and the national tax law, while defending fiscal sovereignty.[133]

This opinion was also formulated in the area of direct taxation, for which the rules of national law were adopted in order to eliminate the iniquitous quantification of the tax base in the tax return procedure.[134] The CJEU acknowledged the legitimacy of the national regulation, when monitoring and control measures and requirements for eliminating tax evasion operations were developed, respecting the non-discrimination between residents and non-residents and the principle of proportionality. Still, the proper evaluation of the degree of proportionality is the most important criterion which often led the CJEU to consider that the domestic law is breaking the European law.

With regards to tax accounting, in particular, it has been noted that the legal framework of a special accounting system for a permanent establishment, in line with the regulation of the Member State where the permanent establishment is located, is a disproportionate rule for the purpose of ensuring tax controls, which would force the foreign company to adopt an excessively expensive organizational level (consisting of both the necessary accounting records for the permanent establishment and the normal business activity), in conflict with the needs of non-discrimination with regard to national resident companies, for which there are only regular accounts (Case C-250/95, Futura Participation SA). There is a legitimate view that the CJEU should return in due course to its more traditional Halliburton approach, when it applied community law to an intra-community transaction between qualified legal persons, even if they were under the joint control of an American parent.[135]

132 Ben J.M. Terra and Wattel Peter, *European tax law hardcover*, Alphen aan den Rijn, Wolters Kluwer, Law & Business, 2008.

133 Ben J.M. Terra and Wattel Peter, *European tax law hardcover*, Alphen aan den Rijn, Wolters Kluwer, Law & Business, 2008,

134 See https://curia.europa.eu/en/content/juris/index.htm for Case 01/28/1992, C-204/90, Bachmann; Case 05/15/1997, C-250/95 Futura Participation SA; Case 8.7.1999, C-254/97 Baxter; Case 28.10.1999, C-55/98 Vestergaard.

135 Servaas Van Thiel, The direct income tax case law of the European court of justice: past, trends and future developments, *Tax Law Review*, 62, 2008, ISSN: 0040–0041, Author/

Furthermore, the national ruling of absolute or even relative assumptions, when they are able to generate discriminatory or restrictive effects for the EU fundamental freedoms, were qualified as inherently disproportionate (C-152/11 Baxter and C-55/98 Vestergaard).[136]

The Court of Justice of the European Union does not appear to provide an exemption,[137] at least in principle, to the risk of tax evasion or from the risk of loss of income due to misinterpretation of fiscal liability by taxpayers, as possible causes for breaches of the EU's fundamental freedoms.[138] However, in the more surprising income tax case-law in early 2000,[139] the CJEU decided to deny EU law benefits to third-country corporate groups, not only by limiting a foreign company from a third country direct access to the European internal market but furthermore, by considering that EU companies which are controlled by non-EU parents could be excluded from the benefits of the treaty, because their common parent would not have access to the treaty.[140]

Contrary to the fact that, in line with the presented case-law, the Court does not accept arguments which are based on purely economic reasons (for example loss of tax revenue) and despite the possible but exceptional application of the limitation of the temporal effects of CJEU judgments, it is suspected that CJEU judges always have in mind the huge sums at stake in direct taxation cases.[141] It is also important to note that a CJEU decision on

---

Editor: New York University School of Law, Publisher: Warren, Gorham & Lamont Series: Current periodical series, Language: English, Country of publication: United States of America.

136 Pietro Boria, *Taxation in European Union*, 2nd ed., Cham, Switzerland, Springer International Publishing, 2017, ISBN 978-3-319-53918-8, ISBN 978-3-319-53919-5 (eBook), doi: 10.1007/978-3-319-53919-5, Library of Congress Control Number: 2017934921.

137 See https://curia.europa.eu/en/content/juris/index.htm for Case 16.7.1998, causa C-264/96, Imperial Chemical Industries; Case 09/21/1999, C-307/97 Saint Gobain; Case 06/06/2000, C-35/98 Verkooijen; Case 8.3.2001, C-397/98 and C-410/98, Metallgesellshaft; Case 09/12/2006, C-196/2004 Cadbury Schweppes.

138 Pietro Boria, *Taxation in European Union*, 2nd ed., Cham, Switzerland, Springer International Publishing, 2017, ISBN 978-3-319-53918-8, ISBN 978-3-319-53919-5 (eBook), doi: 10.1007/978-3-319-53919-5, Library of Congress Control Number: 2017934921.

139 See https://curia.europa.eu/en/content/juris/index.htm for Case C-452/04, Fidium Finanz AG v. Bundesanstalt Fur Finanzdienstleistungsanfsicht.

140 Servaas Van Thiel, The direct income tax case law of the European court of justice: past, trends and future developments, *Tax Law Review*, 62, 2008, ISSN: 0040–0041, Author/Editor: New York University School of Law, Publisher: Warren, Gorham & Lamont Series: Current periodical series, Language: English, Country of publication: United States of America.

141 Katerina Pantazatou, Economic and political considerations of the court's case law post crisis: an exemple from tax law and the internal market, *CYELP*, 9, 77–118, 2013.

the incompatibility of a national tax measure with one of the four freedoms affects national budgets in several ways:

- First, the Member State will have to eliminate the discriminatory provision which was meant to increase state budget revenue, in accordance with Article 260 of the TFEU; this liability further implies that, in order to balance its budget, the particular Member State will either have to reduce spending or increase revenue through other taxes.
- Another budgetary challenge for the Member States arises from the retroactive effect of the CJEU rulings, meaning that the Member States are obliged to reimburse all discriminatory taxes they have already collected, given the actual budget, even though the expenditure took place in an earlier budget period.[142]
- The effect of the CJEU decision is not limited to the defendant Member State, as usually a decision against a particular Member State might generate a flow of similar cases in the same state or versus another Member State.[143]

We observe that the CJEU has denied that the contrast with tax avoidance, which is to be conceived as a special operation dedicated to obtaining an undue tax advantage compared to the general purposes of the national tax system, could be permitted in order to allow distinctions from EU regulations.[144] Indeed, it is common in the case-law of the CJEU that the sole use of tax advantages by taxpayers, attributive to the possibility to choose certain goods for particular transactions, does not qualify as an abusive situation, but when it generates the application of artificial schemes, is designed for obtaining exclusively or as the principle purpose tax benefits.[145]

Another important topic in CJEU rulings proving the changing in sovereignty design for the member States is the state aid. After the recent Commission decisions regarding state aid for some important MNEs (see

142 It was the situation for the Romanian so-called pollution tax, mandatory when registering the ownership for a vehicle; the tax was annulled by the CJEU and the Romanian government had to pay back all the revenue collected for this tax, additional penalties included (see http://curia.europa.eu/juris/liste.jsf?language=en&num=C-402/09 Case Tatu).

143 Katerina Pantazatou, Economic and political considerations of the court's case law post crisis: an exemple from tax law and the internal market, *CYELP*, 9, 77–118, 2013.

144 See https://curia.europa.eu/en/content/juris/index.htm for Case 03/09/1999, C-212/97 Centros; Case 09/30/2003, C-167/2001 Inspire Art; Case 09/12/2006, C-196/2004 Cadbury Schweppes.

145 Pietro Boria, *Taxation in European Union*, 2nd ed., Cham, Switzerland, Springer International Publishing, 2017, ISBN 978-3-319-53918-8, ISBN 978-3-319-53919-5 (eBook), doi: 10.1007/978-3-319-53919-5, Library of Congress Control Number: 2017934921.

Section 3.2.2), the doctrine manifested the opinion that the Commission's points of view are based on an improper application of EU law, and should therefore be overturned by the CJEU, which previously decided that state aid requires an analysis of the criteria of selectivity and of advantage. However, in the rulings for this topic, the Commission seems to have mixed the selectivity and advantage into a single criterion of eligibility, minimizing the selectivity condition, despite the fact that selectivity is both an important element of the state aid jurisprudence and has particular relevance in the case of transfer pricing agreements.[146]

Altogether, it is obvious that the constant application of discriminatory tax measures can only be justified in exceptional cases, when there are essential reasons in the public interest to do so, for example, the necessity to combat tax evasion and avoidance and the demand to comply with the balanced allocation of tax jurisdiction. Eventually, the recent tendency to take into account all clauses of tax treaties that do not fall within the scope of the prohibition of discrimination (hidden sovereignty exception for tax treaties), on the consideration that a taxpayer protected by a tax treaty might never be in a scenario similar to a taxpayer not covered by that special tax treaty (weak substantive argument) is not convincing. Possibly, the CJEU would return to its more traditional opinion that Member States are free to conclude tax treaties and decide on the algorithm for allocating their tax prerogatives, but that tax treaties cannot give rise to or justify incompatible discrimination. Therefore, the substantial tax benefits provided for residents cannot be granted or refused on mutual basis, and under European law, must be granted to all non-resident taxpayers in the same situation as the resident taxpayers.[147]

Furthermore, while recognizing the general right of Member States to adjust their tax obligations in accordance with the particular requirements of domestic law and, in particular, for reasons of simplicity, rationality, and tax effectiveness,[148] the CJEU has argued repeatedly that the singular necessity of the public administration to collect more revenues can never justify a derogation from the basic principles of EU law.[149] On other occasions, the

146 Kyle Richard, Are all tax rulings state aid? Examining the European Commission recent state aid decisions, *Houston Business and Tax Law Journal*, XVIII, ISSN: 1543–2602.

147 Servaas Van Thiel, The direct income tax case law of the European court of justice: past, trends and future developments, *Tax Law Review*, 62, 2008, ISSN: 0040–0041, Author/Editor: New York University School of Law, Publisher: Warren, Gorham & Lamont Series: Current periodical series, Language: English, Country of publication: United States of America.

148 See https://curia.europa.eu/en/content/juris/index.htm for Case 26.1.1999, C-18/95 Terhoeve; Case 16.5.2000, C-87/99 Zurstrassen.

149 Pietro Boria, *Taxation in European Union*, 2nd ed., Cham, Switzerland, Springer International Publishing, 2017, ISBN 978-3-319-53918-8, ISBN 978-3-319-53919-5 (eBook), doi: 10.1007/978-3-319-53919-5, Library of Congress Control Number: 2017934921.

CJEU has ruled out the eligibility of a justification case for the divergence of tax avoidance on the argument of failure to recognize rigorous evidence regarding the risk of tax evasion[150] or due to the lack of proportionality of the internal contrast measures of tax avoidance[151]

The Court has made clear in a strand of judgments which covers many areas of European law, including taxation, that the respect of an anti-abuse doctrine under Community law is deeply related to the purposes of the breached Community rules themselves (i.e., joined Cases C-116/16 and C-117/16,[152] and Case C-6/16[153]). It is the purpose of a provision, which is essential in order to ascertain which transactions are called abusive and which are not. In one of the most recent extensive analyses of this point, Advocate General Maduro has made clear that the application of the anti-abuse doctrine finds its foundation in the "interpretation in conformity with the purpose and objectives of Community law." This holds true both in the field of primary law, most notably the fundamental freedoms, and of secondary law, especially with reference to the directives in the tax sector.[154]

150 See https://curia.europa.eu/en/content/juris/index.htm for Case 07/17/1997, C-28/95 Leur-Bloem.

151 See https://curia.europa.eu/en/content/juris/index.htm for Case 05/15/1997, C-250/95 Futura Participation SA; Case 07/16/1998, C-264/96, Imperial Chemical Industries – ICI.

152 Judgment of the Court (Grand Chamber) from February 26, 2019 in joined Cases C-116/16 and C-117/16, Reference for a preliminary ruling – Approximation of laws – Common system of taxation applicable in the case of parent companies and subsidiaries of different Member States – Directive 90/435/EEC – Exemption of the profits distributed by companies of a Member State to companies of other Member States – Beneficial owner of the distributed profits – Abuse of rights – Company established in a Member State and paying to an associated company established in another Member State dividends all or almost all of which are then transferred outside the European Union – Subsidiary subject to an obligation to withhold tax on the profits at source), available at: https://curia.europa.eu/juris/document/document.jsf?text=anti-abuse%2B&docid=211047&pageIndex=0&doclang=EN&mode=req&dir=&occ=first&part=1&cid=3835925#ctx1, retrieved on October 15, 2021.

153 Judgment of the Court (Sixth Chamber) from September 7, 2017 in Case C-6/16, Eqiom SAS, formerly Holcim France SAS, Enka SA v. Ministre des Finances et des Comptes publics, France. Reference for a preliminary ruling – Direct taxation – Freedom of establishment – Free movement of capital – Withholding tax – Directive 90/435/EEC – Article 1(2) – Article 5(1) – Exemption – Dividends distributed by a resident subsidiary to a non-resident parent company controlled directly or indirectly by one or more residents of third States – Presumption – Fraud, tax evasion and abuse, available at: https://curia.europa.eu/juris/document/document.jsf?text=anti-abuse%2B&docid=194101&pageIndex=0&doclang=EN&mode=req&dir=&occ=first&part=1&cid=3835925#ctx1, retrieved on October 15, 2021.

154 Wolfgang Schoen, *Abuse of rights and European tax law*, available at: www.cambridge.org/core, retrieved on July 23, 2020.

In this situation, the taxpayer's conduct may be qualified as an expression of abuse of right if the transactions show the following elements of qualification:[155]

1 Without prejudice to the formal application of the rules and conditions laid down in EU law and to the transposition in national law, such transactions shall be characterized by the "essential purpose" of obtaining a tax advantage which is contrary to the purpose of EU law.
2 The essential goal of getting tax advantages must be proved by some objective indicators.[156]

The relevant doctrine argued, while analyzing the case-law so far, that the CJEU seems to be determined in considering that the "shopping forum" in terms of group losses is against the balanced allocation of taxing powers or – as in the Krankenheim and Papillon cases – fiscal coherence of the Member States.[157] The coherence principle for fiscal legislation has enlarged the number of potential successful argumentation presented by the Member States, but it made even more difficult the precise delimitation between the mutually accepted justifications (as balanced allocation of taxing powers, danger of losses being used twice and the danger of tax avoidance) and unlawful conduct. The Advocate General Leger in the Cadbury Schweppes litigation explicitly put up his opinion that the fact that a parent company establishes a subsidiary in another Member State for the avowed purpose of enjoying the more favorable tax regime in that state constitutes, in itself, an abuse of freedom of establishment. The CJEU has pointed out the impact of new regulation of the abusive operation, showing that, in reality, if there is any misconduct, it is stated that "the transactions involved must be redefined so as to restore the situation which would have prevailed without the operations carried out by the abusive practice."[158] The CJEU has to determine the failure of the effects of the abuse of law, with consistent

155 See https://curia.europa.eu/en/content/juris/index.htm for Case 02/21/2006, C-255/02, Halifax.

156 Pietro Boria, *Taxation in European Union*, 2nd ed., Cham, Switzerland, Springer International Publishing, 2017, ISBN 978-3-319-53918-8, ISBN 978-3-319-53919-5 (eBook), doi: 10.1007/978-3-319-53919-5, Library of Congress Control Number: 2017934921.

157 The cases considered so far under the group relief "block of cases" amplify the incoherent legal reasoning of the Court and its inability to provide guidelines that would allow for more legal certainty in this area for all the players involved. See for further details Katerina Pantazatou, Economic and political considerations of the court's case law post crisis: an exemple from tax law and the internal market, *CYELP*, 9, 77–118, 2013.

158 See https://curia.europa.eu/en/content/juris/index.htm for Case 02/21/2006, C-255/02, Halifax.

regeneration of the transaction in accordance with the standards of conduct normally applicable.[159]

To synthesize our analysis, it is abuse of right in tax planning in CJEU jurisprudence when circumstances describe EU transactions (Case C-249/17[160] and Case C-48/20[161]), company formation, re-shaping contractual obligation, unlawful relevance of taxpayer's intention. There are justified actions, such as the relevance of free choice in EU law, intention to save taxes, company internal financial efficiency but wholly artificial arrangements, when there are not any real economic activities, should always be regarded as abusive, as they are not within the scope of ruling the European fundamental freedoms of the single market.[162]

Starting with the powerful lines of the case-law prohibiting exit and access restrictions using the direct taxation, it is obvious that any increased taxes on cross-border transaction, by comparison to identical domestic operation are considered discrimination, regardless if they are imposed by the state of origin on persons wishing to be dynamic from the economic point of view and who move to another Member State or by the destination state for those who want access to the European market. In CJEU case-law, precise directions have been developed for interpretation of the European law, for eliminating the possibility to validate exit taxes resulting from the definition

159 Pietro Boria, *Taxation in European Union*, 2nd ed., Cham, Switzerland, Springer International Publishing, 2017, ISBN 978-3-319-53918-8, ISBN 978-3-319-53919-5 (eBook), doi: 10.1007/978-3-319-53919-5, Library of Congress Control Number: 2017934921.

160 Judgment of the Court (First Chamber) from October 17, 2018 in Case C-249/17, Ryanair Ltd v. The Revenue Commissioners, Reference for a preliminary ruling – Common system of value added tax (VAT) – Concept of taxable person – Holding company – Deduction of input tax – Expenditure for consultancy services received for the purpose of the acquisition of another company's shares – Acquiring company's intention to provide management services to the target company – Those services not provided – Right to deduct VAT charged on the services received, available at: https://curia.europa.eu/juris/document/document.jsf?text=U%2Btransactions%2B&docid=206858&pageIndex=0&doclang=en&mode=req&dir=&occ=first&part=1&cid=3842372#ctx1, retrieved on October 15, 2021.

161 Judgment of the Court (Sixth Chamber) from March 18, 2021 in Case C-48/20, UAB 'P.' v. Dyrektor Izby Skarbowej w B., Poland, Reference for a preliminary ruling – Taxation – Common system of value added tax (VAT) – Directive 2006/112/EC – Article 203 – Taxes improperly invoiced – Good faith on the part of the issuer of the invoice – Risk of loss of tax revenue – Obligations of the Member States to provide for the possibility of adjusting tax improperly invoiced – Principles of fiscal neutrality and proportionality, available at: https://curia.europa.eu/juris/document/document.jsf?text=U%2Btransactions%2B&docid=239004&pageIndex=0&doclang=EN&mode=req&dir=&occ=first&part=1&cid=3842372#ctx1, retrieved on October 15, 2021.

162 Wolfgang Schoen, *Abuse of rights and European tax law*, available at: www.cambridge.org/core, retrieved on July 23, 2020.

of taxable income items (capital gains are taxable only on exit), exemptions (only income from exempt domestic sources is taxed), deductible expenses (only internal costs are deductible), rates (higher rates for income from foreign sources or units with foreign capital), tax credits (imputation credits, foreign tax credits and incentive credits), and tax procedures. Meanwhile, powerful directions of interpretation have been derived from the presented CJEU case-law on prohibited access taxes (which also cover definitions of the tax base, rates, credits, and procedures), generating a greater tax burden for permanent units and subsidiaries held abroad, and for frontier workers or professionals (including deductions for personal and family expenses and business expenses).[163]

We also include in our final remarks for this section that a minute decrease of the number of preliminary questions sent by the Member States to the CJEU could determine a more indulgent approach of the European court toward national tax systems. It is obvious that the Court cannot directly influence the number of preliminary rulings, as it may not self-invest with such a case, but the number of solutions in favor of the taxpayer could affect the balance of the collaboration between the national and the European judge and, consequently, the Court's decisions would reflect the reduction in Member States' references.[164]

4.4 Reinforcing European integration using tax regulation

The global COVID-19 pandemic crise has generated two contradictory yet simultaneous reactions, determining both slowness for each collaborative process and revival of the global projects for future successful developments. Especially within EU space, the global challenges have generated additional constraints for the integration process, which had recently suffered many obstructive inputs, from the previous financial crises, to the budgetary entanglements, waves of immigration and BREXIT. In this complicated landscape, it seems rather justified that the integration process slowed down like never before and its reinforcing might be anything but a facile phase. At the EU level, the complexity of the integration process and

163 Servaas Van Thiel, The direct income tax case law of the European court of justice: past, trends and future developments, *Tax Law Review*, 62, 2008, ISSN: 0040–0041, Author/Editor: New York University School of Law, Publisher: Warren, Gorham & Lamont Series: Current periodical series, Language: English, Country of publication: United States of America.

164 Katerina Pantazatou, Economic and political considerations of the court's case law post crisis: an exemple from tax law and the internal market, *CYELP*, 9, 77–118, 2013.

the cooperation between Member States necessarily require the adoption of harmonized tax rules in order for the single market to function properly. A form of tighter fiscal cooperation is inevitable, targeting fiscal harmonization and integration. With regard to direct taxes, in general, limited harmonization is justified in the current context, while avoiding discrimination, double taxation and tax evasion. Equally, closer coordination is needed to counteract the distortions generated by the allocation of resources.

Considering the taxation situations manifested on the European free market in the past and the arguments for the development of the European project, the EU Member States could use tax regulation to relaunch the cooperation among them, in the same manner like they have used the custom union at the beginning of the communities and the progressive tax approximation during the last decades. The path to facilitate greater coordination between Member States describes the scenario for preventing tax avoidance using well-targeted corporate tax reform. Consequently, the EU Member States have taken into consideration important measures aimed at stopping profit shifting and preventing the erosion of national tax bases.[165] Analyzing the previously used mechanisms for further tax integration in the EU, the literature observes the positive results of some solutions, such as Enhanced Cooperation, Soft Law, Indirect Harmonization through EMU Reform Legislation, Non-EU Legislation.[166]

As it has been analyzed in the previous sections of this publication, European fiscal cooperation is framed by the rule of fiscal sovereignty, but it has benefited from the effects of soft law mechanisms, namely the recommendations addressed to the Member States by EU institutions, with regard to the everyday development of the national provisions relating to the taxation of income (especially to the taxation of business income). It is expected that the level of approximation of national legislation generated by the soft law is lower than the harmonization of indirect taxes, and the literature has designated for it the figurative concept of "elastic convergence."[167]

In some situations, the harmonization of EU taxation takes the opposite site from the principle of self-determining the tax system, in order to

165 Alicja Brodzka, Increasing transparency in the European Union: developments of Country-by-Country Reporting, *"Zeszyty Teoretyczne Rachunkowości", Stowarzyszenie Księgowych w Polsce*, 93(149), 9–22, 2017.

166 Anna StingCompany tax integration in the European Union during economic crisis – why and how?, *Erasmus Law Review*, 1, 2014, available at: www.erasmuslawreview.nl/; https://heinonline.org

167 Pietro Boria, *Taxation in European Union*, 2nd ed., Cham, Switzerland, Springer International Publishing, 2017, ISBN 978-3-319-53918-8, ISBN 978-3-319-53919-5 (eBook), doi: 10.1007/978-3-319-53919-5, Library of Congress Control Number: 2017934921.

eliminate the possible mismatches between national taxation systems. In the field literature, the principle of harmonization expresses a "positive taxation," i.e., whether the fiscal power exercised by Member States will be directed toward uniform models and agreed objectives, generally compatible with European Union objectives, as opposed to the principle of non-discrimination and other values, which proves "negative taxation."[168]

The concept of fiscal integration has designed most of the key aspects of the income tax system architecture. The structures of the tax base have been shaped by both negative and positive trends of regulatory mechanisms. Despite the updating of the draft tax base, the level to which these limitations and negotiations took place is surprisingly narrow. Additionally, the Member States manifest a great deal of leeway in deciding how to eliminate discriminatory and selective tax measures, because the income tax rates have kept their autonomy, outside the limit of the European harmonized measures. It is the effect of the lack of provision for revenue taxation in the EU primary law, the aspects being regulated predominantly under the formal sovereignty of the Member States.[169]

As one of the direct results of the LuxLeaks scandal, the European Parliament started an investigation into the tax ruling practices, which was not positively supported by the multinational companies. Eventually, the Parliamentary Commission published a report, proposing a country-by-country reporting system, a common consolidated corporate tax base (CCCTB), increased transparency by Member States, a broader role for the European Commission in reviewing tax ruling practices, and better protections for whistle-blowers.[170] At the same time, the European Commission proposed a measure for the exchange of tax rulings by Member States, which was unanimously approved by Member sSates two days before the Parliamentary Commission published its report. During the European Commission investigations, numerous NGOs have published concerning reports on the tax avoidance practices of multinational enterprises and on the low-tax

168 Pietro Boria, *Taxation in European Union*, 2nd ed., Cham, Switzerland, Springer International Publishing, 2017, ISBN 978-3-319-53918-8, ISBN 978-3-319-53919-5 (eBook), doi: 10.1007/978-3-319-53919-5, Library of Congress Control Number: 2017934921.

169 Jussi Jaakkola, A democratic dilemma of European power to tax: reconstructing the symbiosis between taxation and democracy beyond the state?, *German Law Journal*, 20(5), 660–678, July 2019, doi:10.1017/glj.2019.55

170 *Special Committee of the European Parliament on Tax Rulings and Other Measures Similar in Nature or Effect,* Co-rapporteurs: Elisa Ferreira and Michael Theurer – Report on tax rulings and other measures similar in nature or effect no. 2015/2066, available at www.europarl.europa.eu/doceo/document/A-8-2015-0317_EN.html, retrieved on March 10, 2020.

jurisdictions, before and after the Commission published its Decisions. For example, Oxfam's Tax Battles report ranked the Netherlands, Ireland, and Luxembourg among the world's worst tax havens. The Netherlands ranked as the third, Ireland as the sixth.[171]

Still, fiscal harmonization shows the belief that economic and trade integration is the main driver of political and social integration of a common ideological background, in accordance with the general principles applicable to fiscal issues, namely the acceptance of the values of freedom and economic development of the common market, in line with the principles which guarantee the competitive market.[172]

The actions taken unilaterally by the states are within easy reach, involve less energy and political action for adopting and generate short-term results. Still, the unilateral actions are not preferable on the global context, where the national fiscal systems are easily colliding and the alignment of the provisions is very arguable. In order to achieve the EU tax harmonization objectives, there is a doctrine proposing a Directive on the Allocation of Taxing Rights (ATRiD)[173] that would be the most efficient and widely accepted solution, which could fit best in the framework elaborated by the European Commission in the Action Plan for a Fair and Efficient Corporate Tax System and could happily complete the CC(C)TB Proposal for reinforcing the European measures to fight aggressive tax planning and tax avoidance.

From a wider perspective, ATRiD should be adopted on the respective trend of issuing an increased number of directives for harmonizing direct taxation within the EU, shaping the action of the Member States for the proper functioning of the internal market. It is the case of the two revisions of the Directive parent-subsidiary, ATAD and ATAD II, the Tax Dispute Mechanisms Directive, CCTB, CC(C)TB, and the proposed revision of the Interest and Royalties Directive. Based on all of this, the proposed ATRiD directive could be an efficient legal instrument, by enhancing the framework of the measures for the approximation of the Member States' legal systems in the fiscal area, that directly affect the functionality or operationality of the internal market. In this reasoning, the proposal falls within the scope of article 115 of the TFEU, respecting the sovereignty of the states, but

171 Kyle Richard, Are all tax rulings state aid? Examining the European Commission recent state aid decisions, *Houston Business and Tax Law Journal*, XVIII, ISSN: 1543–2602.

172 Pietro Boria, *Taxation in European Union*, 2nd ed., Cham, Switzerland, Springer International Publishing, 2017, ISBN 978-3-319-53918-8, ISBN 978-3-319-53919-5 (eBook), doi: 10.1007/978-3-319-53919-5, Library of Congress Control Number: 2017934921.

173 Paolo Arginelli, A proposal for harmonizing the rules on the allocation of taxing rights within the European Union and in relations with third countries, *Pistone Pasquale, Part 6 – A Possible Roadmap: European Tax Integration*, 653–694, 2018.

redesigning the cooperation within the EU borders. Furthermore, despite the fact that direct taxation is not within the scope of the European Union's exclusive competences, the proposed ATRiD respects the principle of subsidiarity under article 5(3) of the Treaty on European Union (TEU), because it targets offering a proper response to the obstructive effects on the internal market that could not be satisfactorily addressed in the individual legislative approaches of each Member State.

The literature presents ATRiD potential to properly coordinate the applicable rules in Member States' regulation to avoid antinomies. The ATRiD would not fix the difference in the applicable income tax rates, which would remain within the exclusive competence of EU Member States, except for the establishment of minimum tax rates (ideally between 25% and 30%) for taxation at source of dividends, interest, royalties, and certain types of capital gains (capital gains on financial assets and intangible properties). This would help counteract phenomena of directive and tax-treaty shopping, aimed at channeling income flows through specific Member States for the purpose of avoiding or substantially reducing the tax to be paid in the EU Member State of source.[174]

The design of the actual sovereignty right to rule taxation within EU has evolved together with the fiscal cooperation among Member States. National initiatives of each country could eventually sustain the actual status-quo, which has been applicable for half a century and protects the domestic complete autonomy for ruling taxation, stimulating aggressive tax planning and allowing multiple scenarios for tax avoidance. It is in this way proven that law coordination is a slow process, and past results have been constantly evolving, although not very dynamic, nor particularly ambitious.

One of the steps for tighter fiscal cooperation was directed toward building a fairer and more transparent corporate taxation. The proposal for Country-by-Country Reporting (CbCR) between tax administrations targeted the identified need for transparency between fiscal administrations, aiming at facilitating the exchange of tax-related information regarding the MNEs with activity within the EU territory, regardless of their field of operation, for better results in tax auditing operations. Increased transparency could also help to deter multinationals from engaging in aggressive tax planning schemes.[175]

Country-by-Country Reporting is one of the initiatives of the European package issued in the fight against tax avoidance and evasion which

174 Paolo Arginelli, A proposal for harmonizing the rules on the allocation of taxing rights within the European Union and in relations with third countries, *Pistone Pasquale, Part 6 – A Possible Roadmap: European Tax Integration*, 653–694, 2018.

175 Alicja Brodzka – *Increasing transparency in the European Union: developments of Country-by-Country Reporting*, „Zeszyty Teoretyczne Rachunkowości", Stowarzyszenie Księgowych w Polsce, tom 93 (149), 2017, s. 9–22

explicitly proves the modification of the approach toward corporate taxation. It seems that the overall aim is not limited to protecting national tax bases, but creating a wider fiscal perspective of European market, as a whole.[176] The last decade has brought an intensification of European initiatives aimed at fighting tax avoidance and evasion, i.e., on May 25, 2016, ECOFIN decided on the amendments to the EU Directive on the Automatic Exchange of Information, extending the CbCR scope in respect to the requirements of the Single Market and EU law, yet in line with international actions in fighting Base Erosion and Profit Shifting.[177] There is also the issue of taxing the dividends, which can be treated similarly to the misfunctions arising from the simple interaction of two tax systems within EU, using the different treatment of incoming and outgoing dividends, the choice of the state to offer exemption from double taxation (home – host or none), compatibility with the method of exemption from double taxation (without the possibility of applying both the credit and the exemption methods simultaneously), and subsequently the most desirable neutrality to be achieved.[178]

At the OECD level, the members agreed on 15 actions targeting Base Erosion Profit Shifting (BEPS), including the CbCR for fiscal authorities regarding important financial information about multinationals activity. The European perspective is wider, because implementing Country-by-Country Reporting on the European market in a uniform manner is important, especially if we consider that some states were prepared to adopt the necessary legal provisions in accordance with the OECD BEPS initiative, while some were not willing to implement it at all. Strengthening these requirements in EU law would prevent gaps in the EU's tax transparency network and administrative burdens for businesses.[179]

176 Pierre Moscovici, European Commissioner for Economic and Financial Affairs, Taxation and Customs in office at that time, said at the Tax Congress of the Berlin Tax Forum 2016: *"I must stress that it is not just our Member States that benefit from the new EU approach to corporate taxation. Businesses will benefit too. I want to shatter the myth, that fighting corporate tax avoidance and creating a competitive business environment are mutually exclusive goals. In fact, they are two sides of the same coin*", available at: www.europa-nu.nl/id/vk53kpc3psz8/nieuws/speech_by_commissioner_pierre_moscovici?ctx=vk5qdkqbp5io, retrieved on April 14, 2020.

177 ALICJA BRODZKA – *Increasing transparency in the European Union: developments of Country-by-Country Reporting,* "Zeszyty Teoretyczne Rachunkowości", Stowarzyszenie Księgowych w Polsce, tom 93 (149), 2017, s. 9–22

178 Katerina Pantazatou, Economic and political considerations of the court's case law post crisis: an exemple from tax law and the internal market, *CYELP*, 9, 77–118, 2013.

179 Alicja Brodzka – *Increasing transparency in the European Union: developments of Country-by-Country Reporting,* „Zeszyty Teoretyczne Rachunkowości", Stowarzyszenie Księgowych w Polsce, tom 93 (149), 2017, s. 9–22

In addition to the OECD initiative, EU Directive 2016/881 provides the legal grounds for Member States to implement CbCR between tax authorities, including the possibility to make the CbCR available to the public. However, with regard to the Commission's proposal for a common consolidated corporate tax basis (CCCTB Directive), parliaments have been much more active, which illustrates their strong opposition to more tax harmonization.[180]

The so-called Anti-BEPS Directive 2016/1164/EU aimed at designing harmonized national regulation for the protection of the domestic corporate tax bases. Still, it covered few topics in the targeted field of application, namely interest limitation, exit taxation, a general anti-abuse rule, controlled foreign company rule to deter profit shifting, and a loose rule on hybrid mismatches in the tax treatment of entities or income categories.[181]

The negative effects of the tax system disparities on the internal market are constructively solved when the effective harmonization is accomplished. Moreover, the past decades proved that the European Commission's efforts for various coordinating actions were ineffective or insufficient to erase the negative effects created by the tax rules elaborated individually by the Member States. In response to the obligation to eliminate possible double taxation, the countries tax the profits attributed to subsidiaries and permanent establishments based on unlimited tax liability (subsidiary) or based on limited tax liability (permanent establishment). In either case, the overall profit of a multinational company has to be apportioned to the countries where its subsidiaries or permanent establishments are located.[182]

It was also observed that Member States' unilateral actions to fight effectively against aggressive tax planning are not successful and the international community looked for widely supported actions. It is the justification for G20 and the OECD's launching of the BEPS Project and the EU Council's adoption of the ATAD and double amending the Parent-Subsidiary Directive.[183] One of the current concerns in taxation is the relocation of

180 Anna Sting, Company tax integration in the European Union during economic crisis – why and how?, *Erasmus Law Review*, 1, 2014, available at: www.erasmuslawreview.nl/; https://heinonline.org

181 Thomas Jaeger, Tax concessions for multinationals: in or out of the reach of state aid law?, *Journal of European Competition Law & Practice*, 8(4), 2017.

182 Ulrich Schreiber, *International company taxation: an introduction to the legal and economic principles*, Berlin, Heidelberg, Springer-Verlag, 2013, ISBN 978-3-642-36305-4, doi: 10.1007/978-3-642-36306-1.

183 Paolo Arginelli, A proposal for harmonizing the rules on the allocation of taxing rights within the European Union and in relations with third countries, *Pistone Pasquale, Part 6 – A Possible Roadmap: European Tax Integration*, 653–694, 2018.

companies' headquarters, with the intention to benefit from the residence rights in a low-tax Member State. The exit state is entitled to prescribed exit taxation, which most likely breaks the European law and is likely to be rejected by the Court of Justice of the European Union.[184]

The regulation on common consolidated tax base CC(C)TB in the European Union (EU) will radically change the company's taxation, a necessary measure to diminish aggressive tax planning strategies and eliminate the difficulty in determining transfer pricing. Although the applicability of the territorial source taxation principle will be abolished, the European Commission's proposal for CC(C)TB is welcome in terms of reducing bureaucracy for taxpayers but also for tax authorities.

The EC project allocates the consolidated profits of multinationals based on an apportionment formula, based on the volume of sales, the number of employees, and the capital invested. We estimate that the effects of the proposal, as amended in the European Parliament in March 2018, are even wider than the previewed effects of the recommendations formulated by the OECD. The document incorporating the CC(C)TB proposal is under negotiation and the final text is subject to unanimous approval by the Council of the European Union, the current challenge being to reach the political agreement. Application of the CC(C)TB will redistribute corporate profits in EU Member States, and some of the founding states will suffer tax revenue losses as part of the taxable profits will be allocated to other states. In our opinion, the CC(C)TB project will only succeed if the proposed calculation method is applied globally, as the effects of the new regulation will occur outside the EU borders.[185]

The CC(C)TB represents a comprehensive reform of the current tax regime in the EU, through deeper tax harmonization methods and mechanisms than the international taxation recommendations of the G20 and OECD anti-BEPS initiatives. From a global perspective, the competitive tax environment in the EU could be disadvantaged by the introduction of stricter measures than those recommended by the OECD/BEPS, but the proper functioning of the internal market requires a more comprehensive solution, combating tax evasion. If in the 2011 CCTB project the focus was on the administrative burden and possibly the monitoring of transfer pricing, now the CC(C)TB regulation promotes the mechanism of consolidation and profit sharing for taxation, as a fair and efficient response to the transfer of profits and for limiting aggressive tax planning. The formula for profit

184 Ulrich Schreiber and Gregor Fuhrich, European group taxation-the role of exit taxes, *European Journal of Law and Economics*, 27, 257–274, 2009.

185 Mihaela Tofan – *The challenges in CCTB/CCCTB proposal. From sovereignty to fiscal harmonization within the EU*, in Cluj Tax Forum Journal, no. 5/2019

sharing, which is the key element of CC(C)TB, is quite convincing from a political point of view, and not from an economic point of view, because the principle of taxation of profits at source would have been eliminated. However, due to the difficulty of determining appropriate transfer prices, the change proposed by the EC is welcome.

There are several issues that could be obstacles to the adoption of the CC(C) TB, one of the identified problems being the lack of harmonization of deduction rules, which leads to the establishment of sovereign tax bases by national tax authorities. Therefore, the deduction rules are at least as important as tax rates.

The effects of a single formula on Member States' tax revenues should not be neglected either. Smaller countries will lose some of their tax base, while larger countries would gain from the proposed allocation formula. This makes it extremely complicated to find a sustainable solution in the EU that allows for a level playing field. Loss compensation could be politically appropriate for smaller countries.

The proposed EU regulation for the CC(C)TB is an ambitious and promising goal, which we believe will drive growth in the EU and drive research and innovation. The European Commission's proposal to establish a common corporate tax base aims at ambitious goals, because it significantly reduces both compliance and administrative costs for European groups. Yet, the Commission's proposal to replace separate entity accounting with a profit allocation, considering the specific formula apportionment, raises the issue of a few possible negative effects. The proposed formula for the apportionment of the income takes into consideration the source principle, which may place some Member States in a disadvantaged position, facing losses in both real economic activity and tax revenue. Moreover, anti-avoidance tax rules concerning non-EU countries must be harmonized to prevent negative tax revenue spillover effects.[186]

The Committee on Economic and Monetary Affairs of the European Parliament (ECON committee) adopted its report on CC(C)TB proposal onFebruary 21, 2018 and it expressed the proposal to modify *lege ferenda* text as follows:

- Adding a fourth factor ("data" factor) to the apportionment formula
- Regulating the Commission competence to analyze the effectiveness and efficiency of dispute settlement mechanism between Member States
- Establishing the Commission competence to draw up a transitional compensation mechanism for Member States which potentially lose tax revenue while applying the CCCTB rules

186 Ulrich Schreiber and Gregor Fuhrich, European group taxation-the role of exit taxes, *European Journal of Law and Economics*, 27, 257–274, 2009.

- Canceling specific rules for a particular economy domain (notably shipping companies)
- Clear definition for "consolidated tax base" and analysis of consolidation effect both for taxpayer and fiscal authority
- Tasking the Commission to propose to allocate a part of CCCTB revenue to the EU budget and proportionally reduce their contributions

In 2018, it was estimated that a one year delay to the previous implementation agenda would be sufficient to address all the issues, so the regulation would be adopted and published in/by 2019, application starting by 2020. The failure scenario was less probable in 2018 and it was the moment when the Commission would be requested to issue a completely new proposal, based on Article 116 of the Treaty on the Functioning of the EU (the ordinary legislative procedure). Simultaneously, it was previewed as a last procedural action in the hypothesis of failure that the enhanced cooperation should be initiated by Member States which still believe in the projects and its goals. The content of this report was adopted by the members of the European Parliament in plenary on March 15, 2018, noting that its vote is consultant. The "Common Consolidated Corporate Tax Base" (CCCTB) – part of a wide-ranging proposal to create a single, clear and fair EU corporate tax regime – was backed by MEPs on 15-March-2018 (Thursday) by 438 votes to 145 votes, with 69 abstentions. A separate, complementary measure which creates the basis for the harmonized corporate tax system – the Common Corporate Tax Base – was approved by 451 votes to 141, with 59 abstentions.[187]

Although the previewed deadlines were not respected, the failure of the CC(C)TB proposal was not acknowlegded, because the global COVID-SARS2 pandemic crises emerged in 2019 and it has changed the agenda for every regulatory project, justifying any delays. Consequently, a new proposal was not formulated, yet the previous project did not reach its end.

The draft still under evaluation includes specific provisions for characterizing the "digital presence" in a country, outlining the features considered sufficient to determine taxable profits. The regulation is meant to reduce the gaps in taxation which have permitted digital and global companies to innovate on their tax planning and to diminish in a spectacular way their tax

187 Press release available at: www.europarl.europa.eu/news/en/press-room/20180309IPR99422/meps-approve-new-eu-corporate-tax-plan-which-embraces-digital-presence, retrieved on November 1, 2021.

bills, minimizing the tax liability in the country where they create profits. The European Parliament proposal for CC(C)TB gave specific mandate to the EU Commission to determine the parameters able to characterize digital presence (i.e., number of users, the volume of data collected by digital means). This includes personal data of the users, highly valuable information managed by companies like Facebook, Amazon, and Google (action designated as data mining[188] operations).

The proposal under revision observed the consolidation of the companies' income all over the EU, which are required to calculate their tax bills by adding up the profits and losses of all their European constituent companies. To stop the arbitrary movement of the companies in low-tax jurisdictions, in line with the European freedom of movement on the internal market and freedom of establishment, the consolidation of the resulting profit would then be split for all Member States where the companies' income was generated. It is the first time that the proposal aims at establishing a single set of tax rules that would apply in all Member States, taxpayers complying with a single tax procedure (a one-stop shop)[189] instead of 27 different sets of domestic rules.

Although the proposal was not adopted within the framework of the initially considered agenda, it is still appreciated as a fabulous opportunity to make a giant leap in the field of corporate taxation.[190] The effects of this regulation, when adopted, will generate a new model of taxation, in response to today's digital economy challenges, in response to the unfair tax competition between corporate tax systems within the European single market, by taxing profits inside the jurisdiction where they are actually generated.

There were voices proposing even a tighter integration within the CCTB project, launching the uniform tax rate of 3% for corporate profits, a measure that would bring the European fiscal union much closer to nowadays reality.[191] The report of the European Parliament on the Commission

188 Günther Schuh, Gunther Reinhart, Jan-Philipp Prote, Frederick Sauermann, Julia Horsthofer, Florian Oppolzer, Dino Knoll – *Data Mining Definitions and Applications for the Management of Production Complexity*, Procedia CIRP, Volume 81, 2019, Pages 874–879.

189 OECD (2020), *One-Stop Shops for Citizens and Business, OECD Best Practice Principles for Regulatory Policy*, OECD Publishing, Paris, https://doi.org/10.1787/b0b0924e-en.

190 Draft Report on the proposal for a Council directive on a Common Consolidated Corporate Tax Base (CCCTB), COM(2016)0683 – C8–0471/2016–2016/0336(CNS), Committee on Economic and Monetary Affairs Rapporteur: Alain Lamassoure, available at: www.europarl.europa.eu/doceo/document/ECON-PR-608035_EN.pdf?redirect, retrieved on November 1, 2021.

191 Parlementaire Monitor – *European Parliament rapporteur Paul Tang recommends a 5% tax on digital services*, available at: www.parlementairemonitor.nl/9353000/1/

proposal is still in favor of the threshold of the companies within the scope of the regulation, considering the total turnover greater than €750 million, a protectionist measure to reduce the negative impact on the small companies (start-ups included). European Parliament rapporteur Paul Tang recommended a 5% tax on digital services, in response to the 3% proposed by the Commission, explaining that this change would help to create a "level playing field," by bridging the gap between the taxation rate of traditional and digital enterprises. The Commission based its 3% proposed rate on the statistics of the estimated profits in digital economy, but in the rapporteur's view, it did not consider the actual development of the digital sector in the global economy. When the rate was initially proposed (the European Commission proposed the CCTB project in 2016), a low profitability of 15% for these companies was presumed, while this rate has increased constantly since, to the current profit margin of 25%. For large and renowned digital multinational companies in the field of digital services like Facebook and Google, the profit margins have mounted up to 40%.[192]

This rapporteur proposed five categories of taxable earnings, extending the scope of application of the digital service tax (DST), namely online advertising; intermediation services; the sale of data, video, audio or text content using a digital interface; the sale of goods or services online via e-commerce platforms. The text of the proposal would clearly refer to sale and transmission of data collected from users' active participation in digital interfaces. Rapporteur Tang presented his support for introducing a "sunset clause," echoing the proposal tabled by France,[193] clearly stipulating that the digital service tax proposal refers to temporary measures, pending a permanent solution, and it will be happily replaced by the regulation on significant digital presence, common corporate tax base (CCTB), and consolidation of such a tax (CCCTB). The necessity of a cooperation mechanism between tax authorities when a company collects profits from digital services in many jurisdictions and a revision procedure of the regulation on a regular basis (for instance, to evaluate the scope of application, including the rate, the tax base, the threshold, etc. every three years) is included.

---

j9vvij5epmj1ey0/vksg5vngmwzh?ctx=vhekc59myknp&tab=1&start_tab0=40, retrieved on November 1, 2021.

192 Parlementaire Monitor – *European Parliament rapporteur Paul Tang recommends a 5% tax on digital services*, available at: www.parlementairemonitor.nl/9353000/1/j9vvij5epmj1ey0/vksg5vngmwzh?ctx=vhekc59myknp&tab=1&start_tab0=40, retrieved on November 1, 2021.

193 Deloitte, Proposed digital services tax legislation released, available at: www.taxathand.com/article/11200/France/2019/Proposed-digital-services-tax-legislation-released, retrieved on November 15, 2021.

While the Council has expressed in December 2018 its option for limiting the scope of CC(C)TB proposal application,[194] it observed the Austrian Presidency of the Council of the EU position on the possibility of excluding the sale of data, to the satisfaction of countries such as Germany, and reconfirmed the 2020 timeline for implementing the proposal. Although this timeline could not be accomplished, the action in 2018 and early 2019 proved that both national and EU leaders understand that the current corporate tax system is outdated, and it creates distortions in allocating the corporate tax between concurrent jurisdictions.

The next necessary steps should have been taken by the Council and Commission for their consideration and as to this date, there is no published position of the Council. On May 18, 2021, the Commission adopted a Communication on Business Taxation for the twenty-first century. In it, it notes that a forthcoming proposal, the "Business in Europe: Framework for Income Taxation" (or BEFIT) will provide a single corporate tax rulebook for the EU, based on apportionment and a common tax base.[195] This new proposal will replace the pending proposal of a Common Consolidated Corporate Tax Base (CCCTB), which will be withdrawn and, according to the Communication, the proposal is expected to be tabled in 2023. To ensure effective taxation, the communication launches the idea of the EU tax mix package that would be developed until 2050. It is a more ambitious plan, with a wider timeline but its success must be regarded with prudence, in the context of failure of the CCCTB proposal. The new project is meant to respond to the challenge of the EU budget and the Commission will propose additional new resources, which could include a Financial Transaction Tax and its own resource linked to the corporate sector.

The context of these communications corresponds to digital companies' tendency to assume reduced fiscal liabilities, in comparison with other taxpayers and their option to choose the tax residency to benefit from the low-tax regime, innovating on the tax planning mechanisms. The manifested intention of the European Commission is to prepare a EU corporate tax proposal with a digital levy that will ensure fair contribution of the digital sector to the financing of the recovery in EU and to society at large, after the global pandemic crise. Although the proposal will be technically

194 Council conclusions on the Code of Conduct (Business Taxation), 14363/18 FISC 480 ECOFIN 1058, available at: https://data.consilium.europa.eu/doc/document/ST-15802-2018-INIT/en/pdf, retrieved on November 15, 2021.

195 Available at: https://ec.europa.eu/taxation_customs/system/files/2021-05/communication_on_business_taxation_for_the_21st_century.pdf, retrieved on December 20, 2021.

independent of the forthcoming global agreement on international corporate tax reform, it is previewed that it will be compatible with other international obligations; it will coexist with the implementation of an OECD agreement on sharing a fraction of the taxable base of the largest multinational enterprises, once the latter is ratified and transposed in EU law.

The communication on the future European corporate tax uses extensively the concept of fair taxation and fairness in allocating the taxable revenue between Member States' jurisdictions. The prolonged experience with the CC(C)TB project determined the present option for the simplicity of the following proposal, to facilitate not only the investment and growth, thus reinforcing the Single Market, but also to lead to the Member States' consensus.

Until the European project for all the 27 members takes the necessary steps to advance on the path of fiscal consolidation, integration for corporate tax, and efficient taxation for digital services, unilateral action is free to be manifested as the domestic tax authorities consider most appropriate. One of the recent and powerful unilateral actions is the France initiative for taxing digital services, adopted in 2019, and establishing a tax of 3% for "the supply, by electronic means, of a digital interface that allows users to contact and interact with other users, including for the delivery of goods or services directly between those users" (such as online marketplaces) and "services provided to advertisers or their agents enabling them to purchase advertising space located on a digital interface accessible by electronic means in order to display targeted advertisements to users located in France, based on data provided by such users."[196] Regarding the thresholds and de-minimis provisions, the scope of regulation refers to two criteria, addressing any companies with worldwide revenues of at least EUR 750 million and French local revenues of at least EUR 25 million, including French resident companies and non-resident companies, with and without a French permanent establishment, which means that non-resident entities with French local revenues are in scope. Avoiding possible double taxation effects, the provision stated that the digital service tax should be deductible from corporate income tax that is paid in France, but the tax should not fall within the scope of the double tax treaties. There are legal uncertainties on how this limitation will be served, as foreign companies without French permanent establishment are subject to the tax.

196 BDO Global – France – Digital Services Tax, available at: www.bdo.global/en-gb/microsites/digital-services-taxation/countries-cit-map/france-digital-services-tax, retrieved on November 1, 2021.

The Digital Services Tax (DST) has been dubbed as the "GAFA tax" (an acronym of the main US targets: Google, Apple, Facebook, and Amazon)[197] yet it applies not only to US MNEs but also to other international groups from China, Germany, Spain, and even France, the French tax administration estimating around 30 international groups under the scope of the provision. Actually, in response to the numerous opponents of this unilateral regulation, the tax was suspended to leave room for mutual agreements on the topic. Since no agreement has been reached at the OECD on the taxation of the digital economy, the Minister of Economy announced that France would apply the Digital services Tax as from December 2020. Since the regulation came into force in France, the tax has brought in €375 million euros to the French Treasury in 2020, €358 million in 2021 and €518 million are estimated for 2022.

Legitimate concerns about the effects of the French digital service tax globally led the G20 group to reach an agreement concerning the international tax, in July 2021. However, as the agreement is not yet implemented, the French Minister of Economic Affairs has stated that the digital service tax will be maintained in France and the multilateral agreement on this topic, endorsed by the OECD, will probably be applicable starting 2023.[198]

To summarize the European Union struggle to identify efficient regulation for corporate taxation, we note that both the Council and the European Commission proved their option for coordinated if not uniformed legal response to the global challenges in the digital economy. Still, there are difficulties in reaching the consensus of the Member States within the European internal market, and the OECD multilateral project is not evolving with improved speed. Both these conducts in the international taxation have supported the unilateral action of the states, at least until multilateral consensus is achieved.

As stated before in this work, these proposals require unanimity not only at OECD level, but also for the EU Member States, where new fiscal regulations are adopted unanimously. The fiscal proposal for regulation in EU did not evolve as intended and regarding the digital service tax, there are already negative opinions presented by some Member States. The main formulated step back points address the nature of the digital service tax, which is ruled like an income tax, meaning that its collection must take

197 Sophie Dorin – *Digital Services Tax in France,* October 2021, available at: www.twobirds.com/en/news/articles/2019/global/digital-services-tax-in-france, retrieved on December 20, 2021.

198 G20 to back global corporate tax deal, says French finance minister, available at: www.reuters.com/business/g20-back-global-corporate-tax-deal-says-french-finance-minister-2021-07-06/, retrieved on December 20, 2021.

place even for a company which has losses, and the lack of the tax credit mechanism for digital service tax, with the direct effect that the tax cannot be deducted from the corporate income tax paid in the state where the company is incorporated.

Another important issue regarding the European proposal for a digital service tax is the reaction of the United States, as the European Commission estimates that about 120–150 companies will fall within the scope of the new rules, half of which are expected to be located in the United States, and only a third in the EU. At the meeting of G20 leaders on Summit in 2018 in Buenos Aires, the United States has already expressed concerns and may decide to take defensive measures, if the EU should adopt these proposals.[199]

Mandated by the G20, the OECD groups of experts are working on a global consensus- based solution to reform the international corporate tax framework. As we have stated before, the discussions in the Inclusive Framework focused on two broad work streams: Pillar One (new nexus and innovative formula for allocation the taxing rights) and Pillar Two (minimum effective taxation of multinationals' profits). Although they seem to be independent and the negotiation between interested Member States evolved differently, the two proposals are interconnected, both addressing the increasing globalization and digitalization of the economy.

The current proposal under Pillar One includes new international rules on the taxation of corporate profits to reflect the changing nature of business models, in response to the developing digital economy, where the companies generate profit without a physical presence. It will give market jurisdictions a right to tax part of the profits of certain non-resident businesses by providing for a reallocation of a portion of these global profits among the jurisdictions where the group has customers or users, using an agreed formula. In the first draft of the proposal, the regulation in Pillar One aimed the business with digital activity, and the actual proposal includes the largest and most profitable MNEs, from any sector of economic activity.

The proposal in Pillar Two responds to the unfair tax competition, establishing a minimum level of tax, regardless of which Member State is entitled to collect tax, discouraging the MNEs to change the location of their activity in order to submit to a more favorable fiscal regulation. It is intended that rules in Pillar Two from the OECD proposals determine the alignment of the tax liability to a certain previewed level, still not eliminating the

199 See par. 26 from G20 Leaders' Declaration: Building Consensus for Fair and Sustainable Development, December 1, 2018, available at: www.g20.utoronto.ca/2018/2018-leaders-declaration.html, retrieved on December 20, 2021.

national possibility to rule the other characteristics of their tax systems. The intention is to limit if not eliminate the tax avoidance opportunities, so easy to utilize in the global digital economy.

It is important to observe that the EU actions to respond to the necessity of the corporate tax reform in the global digital economy are in line with the OECD initiatives. Both pillars of the future global agreement under evaluation within the OECD are similar to the European Commission's communication from 2021 for a business taxation framework in the twenty-first century.[200] Both proposals include solutions for allocation of profits of MNEs in the present context and they both are slowly advancing.

While the European Commission is assuming the diligent part in the international discussions, simultaneously it supports the Member States to identify and reach the consensus for the most efficient possible regulation at this point within the European internal market. In its conclusions of March 25, 2021, the European Council also reiterated "its strong preference for and commitment to a global solution," and stated that it would strive to reach a consensus-based solution by mid-2021 within the framework of the OECD.[201] The term was once more not respected, and the Council confirmed that the European Union will be ready to move forward if the prospect of a global solution is not forthcoming. We recall that, as a basis for an additional own resource, the Commission will put forward in the first semester of 2021 a proposal on a digital levy, with a view to its introduction at the latest by January 1, 2023.

A new deadline could not be established without assuming the possibility that the global agreement is adopted sooner, so rules for its implementation within the EU are required. Under the rules of the international law, the multilateral convention of OECD will translate into mandatory the application of the provisions in Pillar One and Pillar Two for participating countries, some of them Member States of the EU. In order to ensure its consistent implementation in all EU Member States, including those that are not members of the OECD and do not participate in the Inclusive Framework, the Commission will use the mechanisms of the EU secondary law, namely the Directive, for the implementation of the multilateral agreement on the internal market. There will be some interactions between the

200 Communication from the Commission to the European Parliament and the Council, *Business taxation for the 21st century,* Brussels, May 18, 2021, available at: https://ec.europa.eu/taxation_customs/system/files/2021-05/communication_on_business_taxation_for_the_21st_century.pdf, retrieved on November 1, 2021.

201 See par. 6 g) from the Statement of the Members of the European Council, Brussels, March 25, 2021, available at: www.consilium.europa.eu/media/48976/250321-vtc-euco-statement-en.pdf, retrieved on November 15, 2021.

existent EU regulation on the previewed topics and the multilateral agreement, the European Commission already considering means of action for solving these situation.[202]

Implementation of Pillar Two, as it is included in the OECD initiative, will interact with the existing rules in the ATAD directive, specifically for the Controlled Foreign Company (CFC) rules. Also the pending European project to adopt a Directive to eliminate withholding tax obstacles to cross-border interest and royalty payments will interact with the primary rule under Pillar Two, supporting the agreement on the proposal for a group of companies and establishing a minimum level of tax in the destination state, a pre-condition for benefiting from the absence of withholding tax.

As stated in the Communication on Tax Good Governance in the EU and Beyond,[203] the Commission will propose to introduce Pillar Two in the criteria used for assessing third countries in the EU listing process, so as to incentivize them to join the international agreement. The solution is accordingly the EU's expressed opinion for promoting internationally agreed good practices.

Still, as it was previewed in the CC(C)TB proposal, the actual direction of action for the EU ismeant to go beyond the OECD agreement with some targeted solutions. The declaration of the European Commission for May 18, 2021 established the EU's business tax agenda for the next two years, with measures that improve the current system, focusing on the dual priorities of ensuring fair and effective taxation and promoting productive investment and entrepreneurship.[204]

In order to provide fair and effective taxation, the European Commission proposed as the first step a greater public transparency on the taxes paid by large economic actors, a direct response to the rising demand from citizens and civil society organizations to ensure more transparency and fairness in business taxation, aiming specifically at corporate income taxation. For this purpose, the Commission committed to prepare a new proposal for the

202 See box 2, page 6 in the Communication from the Commission to the European Parliament and the Council, *Business Taxation for the 21st Century*, Brussels, 18 of May 2021, available at: https://ec.europa.eu/taxation_customs/system/files/2021-05/communication_on_business_taxation_for_the_21st_century.pdf, retrieved on November 1, 2021.

203 Communication from the Commission to the European Parliament and the Council on Tax Good Governance in the EU and beyond, Brussels, July 15, 2020, available at: https://ec.europa.eu/taxation_customs/system/files/2020-07/2020_tax_package_tax_good_governance_communication_en.pdf, retrieved on December 20, 2021.

204 See page 9–10 in the Communication from the Commission to the European Parliament and the Council, Business Taxation for the 21st Century, Brussels, 18 of May 2021, available at: https://ec.europa.eu/taxation_customs/system/files/2021-05/communication_on_business_taxation_for_the_21st_century.pdf, retrieved on November 1, 2021.

annual publication of the effective corporate tax rate of certain large companies with operations in the EU, using the methodology agreed for the OECD Pillar Two methodology for establishing the tax level. The effective corporate tax rate provides information regarding the proportion of corporate tax paid by companies relative to the amount of profits they generate rather than relative to their "taxable profits," which can be reduced through various means such as tax allowances. Hence, the proposal will improve public transparency around the real effective tax rate experienced by large EU companies.

It is mandatory that the EU takes further actions to implement the minimum level of taxation, for instance against the abusive use of shell companies[205](i.e., companies with no or minimal substantial presence and real economic activity – through a new legislative initiative to neutralize the misuse of shell entities for tax purposes. While several actions at the EU and international level provide instruments to tackle the use of abusive tax structures, legal entities with no or only minimal substance and economic activity continue to pose a risk of being used for improper purposes, such as aggressive tax planning, tax evasion, or money laundering. There can be valid reasons for the use of such entities, yet there is a need for further action to tackle entities and structures created for the main purpose of reducing the tax liability or disguising improper conduct of the group or operations they belong to, without substance and real economic activities in the countries where they are incorporated.

It is the explicit intention of the Commission proposal to encompass actions such as the obligation for the companies to report to the tax administration the necessary information to assess whether they have substantial presence and real economic activity, denying tax benefits linked to the existence or the use of abusive shell companies, and creating new tax information, monitoring and tax transparency requirements. The Commission also intends to take further steps to prevent royalty and interest payments leaving the EU from escaping taxation (so-called "double non-taxation")[206].

205 Pinto Nogueira, João Félix, Pasquale Pistone, Ivan Lazarov and Alessandro Turina, Abuse through the Use of Shell Companies and Arrangements for Tax Purposes in the European Union: Feedback on the EU Consultation by the IBFD Task Force on EU law, *Intl. Tax Stud*, 4(7), July 14, 2021, Journal Articles & Opinion Pieces IBFD, available at: https://ssrn.com/abstract=, retrieved on December 20, 2021.

206 Christoph Marchgraber, *'The Avoidance of Double Non-taxation in Double Tax Treaty Law: A Critical Analysis of the Subject-To-Tax Clause Recommended by the European Commission'*, (2014), 23, EC Tax Review, Issue 5, pp. 293–302, available at: https://kluwerlawonline.com/journalarticle/EC+Tax+Review/23.5/ECTA2014027, retrieved on January 15, 2022.

In parallel, the Commission will continue to use all tools at its disposal to ensure companies pay their fair share of tax, including the enforcement of state aid rules. While direct taxation falls within the competence of Member States, Member States must exercise that competence consistently with Union law, including State aid rules.

In summary, the European Commission assumed actions to ensure fair and effective taxation referring to:

- Action 1: Table a legislative proposal for the publication of effective tax rates paid by large companies, based on the methodology under discussion in Pillar Two of the OECD negotiations (by 2022)
- Action 2: Table a legislative proposal setting out union rules to neutralize the misuse of shell entities for tax purposes (by Q4 2021)

As a second line of action, the Commission aims at enabling productive investment and entrepreneurship.[207] The fiscal policy plays an important role in influencing businesses conduct, namely the option to invest on a certain market and to establish (or not) a permanent location.[208] This influence of tax policy on the economic growth is more apparent during post crises recovery, as the economy will evolve post COVID-19 pandemic. It is the determinant of the many Member States' actions to relieve the immediate tax burden on SMEs, for example via deferral of tax obligations. Still, there are many different tax rules in Member States with string influence on the business conduct to determine economic recovery and growth, namely the treatment of losses. In order to provide fair competition for the companies within the European internal market, the Commission issued a recommendation to Member States on the domestic treatment of losses, benefiting especially SMEs,[209] proposing loss carry back, for its advantage of benefitting only the businesses that were profitable in the years before the pandemic, which means that it would support healthy businesses as a matter of principle.

207 See p. 3.2, page 10 in the Communication from the Commission to the European Parliament and the Council, Business Taxation for the 21st Century, Brussels, May 18, 2021, available at: https://ec.europa.eu/taxation_customs/system/files/2021-05/communication_on_business_taxation_for_the_21st_century.pdf, retrieved on November 1, 2021.

208 M. Bonucchi, M. Ferrari, S. Tomasini and T. Tsenova, Tax policy, investment decisions and economic growth, *Revue de l'OFCE*, 141, 225–2622015, doi:10.3917/reof.141.0225

209 European Commission Recommendation (EU) 2021/801 of May 18, 2021 on the tax treatment of losses during the COVID-19 crisis, published in the Journal of the European Union L 179/10 from May 20, 2021, available at: https://eur-lex.europa.eu/legal-content/EN/TXT/PDF/?uri=CELEX:32021H0801&from=EN, retrieved on November 15, 2021.

The doctrine assessed that the tax framework allowing for a tax deduction of interest on debt determines persisting pro-debt bias of tax rules.[210] In other words, a company is entitled to deduct interests from debt financing, while the costs related to an equity financing (i.e., payment of dividends) are not deductible. In this line, the company is encouraged to finance investments through debt rather than by equity. In time, this conduct will determine growing volume of debts, resulting eventually in insolvency and negatively influencing the European internal market. It is the European Commission's statement that this issue has become more pressing, as the stock of debts of companies has increased significantly due to the economic crisis following the COVID-19 pandemic, assuming that it will make a proposal to address the debt-equity bias in corporate taxation, via an allowance system for equity financing, thus contributing to the re-equitization of financially vulnerable companies.[211] The proposal will incorporate anti-abuse measures to ensure it is not used for unintended purposes and the previewed actions to enable productive investment and entrepreneurship are:

- Adopt a recommendation on the domestic treatment of losses (already accomplished[212])
- Make a legislative proposal creating a Debt Equity Bias Reduction Allowance (DEBRA), undergoing for the first semester of 2022[213]

The European Commission action is intended to go beyond the OECD agreement with the agenda for EU Business taxation environment for the twenty-first century. The European Commission acknowledges that

210 Jeff Gordon, Coherent capital structure policy: between bailouts and the interest deduction, *Yale Law School*, 1182–1211, 2021, available at: https://openyls.law.yale.edu/bitstream/handle/20.500.13051/8342/09._Gordon_Note._Final._1182_1225.pdf?sequence=2&isAllowed=y, retrieved on January 15, 2022.

211 See page 11 in the Communication from the Commission to the European Parliament and the Council, Business Taxation for the 21st Century, Brussels, May 18, 2021, available at: https://ec.europa.eu/taxation_customs/system/files/2021-05/communication_on_business_taxation_for_the_21st_century.pdf, retrieved on November 1, 2021.

212 European Commission Recommendation (EU) 2021/801 of May 18, 2021 on the tax treatment of losses during the COVID-19 crisis, published in the Journal of the European Union L 179/10 from May 20, 2021, available at: https://eur-lex.europa.eu/legal-content/EN/TXT/PDF/?uri=CELEX:32021H0801&from=EN, retrieved on November 15, 2021.

213 The Debt-equity bias reduction allowance (DEBRA) initiative is under public consultation, information, available at: https://ec.europa.eu/info/law/better-regulation/have-your-say/initiatives/12995-Debt-equity-bias-reduction-allowance-DEBRA-_en, retrieved on January 20, 2022.

the global multilateral regulation will constitute a historic step forward toward the modernization of global business tax rules.[214] In consideration of the established threshold, the global agreement on Pillar One, when adopted, will initially impact a limited number of companies, from 139 jurisdictions, with substantially different legal framework and various economic pattern. The effect of the global multilateral regulation will be enhanced on the European single market, benefiting from the integration functional mechanisms of tight cooperation between the Member States.

During 2021, the European Commission admitted the difficulties in adopting a common corporate tax system in the single market and its negative effect on competitiveness. Many disadvantages are generated or maintained by the CCCTB project's lack of development and they can and shall be addressed by a new proposal. The Commission committed to propose a new framework for income taxation for businesses in Europe (Business in Europe: Framework for Income Taxation or BEFIT).

BEFIT is a new ambitious project, replacing the CCCTB proposal, which is conceived as a single corporate tax rulebook for the EU, based on the key features of a common tax base and the allocation of profits between Member States based on a formula (formulary apportionment). We observe that the main features of the CCCTB proposal are still on the table, yet it is not the first time when the European legal order moves forward with a proposal that reiterates the content of a previous unsuccessful one, presented in a more attractive and convincing manner. It is expected that the BEFIT proposal will consider the good practice identified in previous negotiation and respect the lines of the global multilateral actions so far, as the formula for the reallocation of profits is included in Pillar One, and rules for calculating the tax base are included in Pillar Two.

It is previewed that the BEFIT proposal will provide simplicity for the companies acting within the European single market, guaranteeing the freedom of movement and establishment as before and submitting to a single regulatory system at least in corporate tax field, not to the 27 different fiscal systems. The tax barriers will be eliminated, and Member States will be able to raise revenue to fund national spending priorities. The simplification will include both substantial and procedural regulation, as the previous

214 See p. 4, page 11 in the Communication from the Commission to the European Parliament and the Council, Business Taxation for the 21st Century, Brussels, May 18, 2021, available at: https://ec.europa.eu/taxation_customs/system/files/2021-05/communication_on_business_taxation_for_the_21st_century.pdf, retrieved on November 1, 2021.

proposals for a common consolidated corporate tax did. According to the European Commission statement,[215] the immediate BEFIT proposal will:

- Create a common rulebook for groups of companies operating in the single market in more than one Member State, reducing barriers to cross-border investment
- Reduce red tape and cut compliance costs in the single market, thereby lessening the administrative burden on tax authorities and taxpayers
- Combat tax avoidance, and support job creation, growth, and investment
- Provide a simpler and fairer way to allocate taxing rights between Member States
- Ensure reliable and predictable corporate tax revenues for Member States

In a few words, the BEFIT proposal will consolidate the profits of the EU members of a multinational group into a single tax base, which will then be allocated to Member States using a formula, to be taxed at national corporate income tax rates. The proposal should pay consideration to sales by destination, reflecting the importance of the location in which the MNEs activity is focused, putting in the same analysis the assets (including intangibles) and labor (personnel and salaries), thus insuring a justified distribution of corporate tax revenue between EU Member States.

The necessity to apply complex transfer pricing rules within the EU will be removed by the use of a formula to allocate profits, which is a new measure within the internal market, but it will be built on the good practice already available. For example, in the US, Canada, and Switzerland, a formula is used to compute the tax base at regional or subnational level. While the principles of a common tax base and of formulary apportionment already featured in the previous CCCTB proposal, the new proposal will reflect the significant changes in the economy and in the international framework since March 2011 when the CCCTB was originally proposed. Most notably, it will build on the approach taken in the forthcoming global agreement in its proposals for the definition of the tax base. It will also feature a different apportionment formula, which will better reflect the realities of today's economy and global developments, in particular by taking better account of digitalization.

215 See page 12 in the Communication from the Commission to the European Parliament and the Council, Business Taxation for the 21st Century, Brussels, May 18, 2021, available at: https://ec.europa.eu/taxation_customs/system/files/2021-05/communication_on_business_taxation_for_the_21st_century.pdf, retrieved on November 1, 2021.

The Commission will work closely with Member States in the preparation of this proposal, also taking into account the views of the European Parliament, and in consultation with the business sector and civil society groups. The BEFIT is expected by 2023.[216]

216 See p. 5 Conclusion, page 11 in the Communication from the Commission to the European Parliament and the Council, Business Taxation for the 21st Century, Brussels, May 18, 2021, available at: https://ec.europa.eu/taxation_customs/system/files/2021-05/communication_on_business_taxation_for_the_21st_century.pdf, retrieved on November 1, 2021.

5 Conclusions and limits of the research

As our analysis points out, the continuous increase of the public spending asks for corresponding enlargement of the public revenue and the regulation to limit and, if possible, to eliminate tax avoidance by multinational companies is a priority both globally and for every state. The issue is yet on debate in the USA, when companies collect income in several states. The difficulties in establishing the taxation system entitled to collect taxes from revenue in digital trade over the frontiers of a particular state is another European and global challenge. Also, the fight against tax avoidance has been within the area of concern for OECD and EU, simultaneously.

The need for harmonized regulation in the tax sector within EU, if not uniform regulation, is supported by our work; the EU legislative actors have already issued some proposals for consolidating the profits of the companies which operate in many Member States, addressing the allocation of the profits in accordance with specific criteria (situ taxation, virtual presence, employment, and number of consumers, volume of transferred data, etc.). The subject is addressed globally by current proposals to adopt a new concept of nexus, the OECD members analyzing the possibility and the effects of this new doctrine, while for the EU Member States and the US literature the characteristics of the new nexus raise critiques and require further clarifications.

The analysis undertaken in this study shows that currently the EU law seems to facilitate tax avoidance by both EU and non-EU taxpayers, rather than prevent this phenomenon. While some literature considers that EU is close to achieving a truly tangible shift toward an effective prevention of tax avoidance under EU law, so that the internal market functions properly, ensuring optimal and fair allocation of resources within the EU, there are serious impediments for the fiscal integration within the internal market.

The EU primary law respects the sovereign right of the Member States to regulate the fiscal system, a situation which favors a unilateral approach toward new regulation in this field, despite the multiple possible negative

DOI: 10.4324/9781003309970-5

side effects, contrary to the fundamental principles of the European internal market (i.e., France regulation for taxing the revenues from digital activities). The status of primary rule of European law for national fiscal sovereignty should not be considered opinionated or an insulated attitude of nation-states, but as the performance power mechanism of the national constitutions, pending the completion of institutional processes aimed at constructing the full integration process. Actually, claiming that the national fiscal power is one of the strongest protected values of the national democratic constitutions.

In this regulatory landscape, the formal European fiscal integration seems to be rather a long-time project, as the Member States have decided to cherish their sovereign right to rule taxation, especially in the present challenging pandemic times. For the time being, the legal tool to be most frequently used while addressing tax issues within EU is the directive, and not the regulation, respecting the state sovereign right to decide how to transpose a particular fiscal goal in the national legal framework. Furthermore, the domain of regulating direct taxation, one of the most important fiscal areas in the contemporary tax system, is mainly addressed within the EU through the tools of the negative integration, which supports the assumption that EU legal order benefits from soft law and indirect legal effect, not only from using the formal strict regulation. There are many activity sectors where the public conduct is already similar or at least approximated, despite the lack of formal coordination by the rule of law. Multiple actions taken by the states in harmonizing their internal legislation to align the fiscal conduct prove that the concept of fiscal sovereignty was reshaped in order to respond to the current demands of cooperation on the internal market.

The harmonization is described in fiscal matters as a positive guiding principle, that is intended to establish a system of law characterized by gradual integration of the national tax systems. The design of a common and unified model of taxation within the EU and the removal of the gap between national fiscal laws are factors for clustering and approximating the national legal systems, with regard to the power to impose taxes.

The Court of Justice of the European Union has a very important role to play in the interpretation and development of EU law in general, and in the development of EU rules in the field of taxation, in particular. The Court has had a traditional moderate and prudential approach, reflected in most of its judgments, also influenced by the necessity to take into consideration the huge impact of its ruling in fiscal cases on the national public budget, directly, and on the European budget, indirectly. In any particular tax situation, the primary effects are for the participant Member States, but the power of the CJEU ruling will mandatorily expand its effect on any other comparable situation within the EU. At the same time, the indirect budgetary effects might spread to the level of the European citizens' level of living.

There is a constant concern of the Member States' regulatory institutions to designing effective controlled foreign companies' rules, respecting their compatibility with EU law. The national legislative organisms have to find the right rules to fight the taxpayers' abusive practices within the EU, while respecting their compliance with the EU primary sources of law. The individual approach toward this goal is often sanctioned by the European Commission or by the CJEU, so the need to cooperate arose naturally and evolved to the current level of coordination of the fiscal regulation, maintaining the rule of unanimity when adopting a particular tax measure in the Council. The sovereign right to rule taxation is still protected by the Member States and it is expressly previewed in the EU primary law, as all Member States are willing to preserve their right to rule taxation for an unlimited time. Still, they are simultaneously obliged to respond to the everyday challenges of harmonizing their taxation, in accordance with the fundamental rules of functioning of the internal market. Their regulation has to address properly the tax avoidance conduct by applying uniform rules. All individual regulatory actions in the fiscal area of the Member States may significantly enhance the collaborative and common approach of various states across the world in preventing tax avoidance, redesigning the concept of sovereignty at least for the EU Member states, if not globally.

If we accept that sovereignty in taxation is untouchable and a state's right to decide completely autonomously on the public revenue is fundamental value for the tax systems, then our study confirms the hypothesis that the unilateral regulation in the tax field is still the formal legitimate method to rule today. Also, in response to the objectives of the research, other features and parameters were highlighted, justifying the approximation of the national tax systems. There are informal challenges in the adoption of EU tax legislation, particularly serving the sovereignty rule. The post-Lisbon EU law includes evidence for the tax uniform policy regime and, undoubtedly, there is a wide acknowledged goal to cooperate among the EU fiscal authorities for tax policymaking. The unique legislative fiscal regulation is possible only when the proper respect is paid to the unanimity rule, while European tax law is indeed building up a new legal environment using two different paths (i.e., positive and negative integration) at an unprecedented speed.

The global action in adopting multilateral regulation addressing the tax avoidance at the international level evolved hand in hand with European initiatives for the same goals, at the beginning of 2022 the OECD proposal showing more certainty for coming into force and with a more accurate agenda. If adopted, the forthcoming global agreement will mark a decisive step forward in the reform of the international corporate tax system, addressing important challenges related to the allocation of taxing rights and minimum effective taxation at global level. The European institutions have already expressed their intentions to take similar ambitious measures at the EU level, building on this progress a fair and effective taxation and that would support productive investment and entrepreneurship. A proposal for Business in Europe: Framework for Income Taxation (BEFIT), was issued for moving toward a common tax rulebook and providing for fairer allocation of taxing rights between Member

We are moving toward European fiscal integration toward a better functioning single market, a legal framework in which Member States will act gradually self-deprived of their national tax sovereignties and European nationals will enjoy a full and immediate protection of their individual rights, under the jurisdiction of the Court of Justice of the European Union, with limited space for tax arbitrage and a substantial simplification of issues raised by cross-border taxation, both within Europe and in the relations with third countries.

If symbiosis will not be achieved by European primary law or through favorable regulatory frameworks, then it is our conclusion that the unilateral regulation will lead the integration process. The sovereign right to rule taxation, protected in the national constitution, will no longer be justified, in connection to the precise provision in the national tax system which will have moved and will evolve toward a unified approach.

Bibliography

Alexy, Robert, Constitutional rights and proportionality, *Journal for Constitutional Theory and Philosophy of Law*, 22, 2014, available at: http://journals.openedition.org/revus/2783; doi: 10.4000/revus.2783

Almendral, Violeta Ruiz, Tax avoidance and the European court of justice: what is at stake for European general anti-avoidance rules?, *Intertax*, 33(12), 560–582, 2005.

Andersen, Torben M. and Maibom, Jonas, *The big trade-off between efficiency and equity – is it there?*, 2016, available at: www.nbs.rs/internet/latinica/90/90_9/TorbenAndersen_wp.pdf

Arginelli, Paolo, A proposal for harmonizing the rules on the allocation of taxing rights within the European Union and in relations with third countries, *Pistone Pasquale, Part 6 – A Possible Roadmap: European Tax Integration*, 653–694, 2018.

Bartelson, J., *A genealogy of sovereignty (Cambridge studies in international relations)*, Cambridge, Cambridge University Press, 1995, doi: 10.1017/CBO9780511586385.

Bartelson, Jens, The concept of sovereignty revisited, *The European Journal of International Law*, 17(2), 463–474, 2006, doi: 10.1093/ejil/chl006

Bonucchi, M., Ferrari, M., Tomasini, S. and Tsenova, T., Tax policy, investment decisions and economic growth. *Revue de l'OFCE*, 141, 225–262, 2015, doi:10.3917/reof.141.0225

Boria, Pietro, *Taxation in European Union*, 2nd ed., Cham, Switzerland, Springer International Publishing, 2017, ISBN 978-3-319-53918-8, ISBN 978-3-319-53919-5 (eBook), doi: 10.1007/978-3-319-53919-5, Library of Congress Control Number: 2017934921.

Brodzka, Alicjia, Increasing transparency in the European Union: developments of country-by-country reporting, *"Zeszyty Teoretyczne Rachunkowości", Stowarzyszenie Księgowych w Polsce*, 93(149), 9–22, 2017.

Brown, Patricia, *OECD update*, STEP Miami 4th Annual Summit, Coral Gables, University of Miami School of Law, May 31, 2013.

Bufan, Radu, *Treaty of tax law – vol. i general theory of taxation*, Bucharest, Hamangiu Publishing House, 2016.

Buhrle, Anna Theresa and Spengel, Christoph, *Tax law and the transfer of start-up losses: a european overview and categorization*, Discussion Paper No. 19–037 | 09/, Berlin, Leibniz Association, ZEW, 2019.

Craig, Paul, *De Burca, Graine – EU Law – Texts, Cases and Material*, 5th ed., New York, Oxford University Press Inc., 2011.

Deak, Daniel, Legal considerations of tax evasion and tax avoidance (September 12, 2009), *Society & Economy*, 26(1), 41–85, 2004, available at: https://ssrn.com/abstract=1472508

Dean, Steven, *A constitutional moment in cross-border taxation*, paper presented in Tax Policy Colloquium, NYU Law School, New York, August 25, 2020.

de Colle, Simone and Bennett, Anne Marie, State-induced, strategic, or toxic? In ethical analysis of tax avoidance practices, *Business & Professional Ethics Journal*, 33(1), 53–82, 2014.

de la Feria, Rita, Tax fraud and selective law enforcement, *Journal of Law ans Society*, 1–31, 2020, ISSN: 0263–323X.

Delimatsis, Panagiotis and Herger, Nils, *Financial regulation at the crossroads: implications for supervision, institutional design and trade*, Alphen aan den Rijn, Kluwer Law International, 2011.

Delors, Jacques, *Report on economic and monetary union in the European Community*, presented (commonly called the delors plan or report) by committee for the study of economic and monetary union, EU Commission – working document, April 17, 1989, available at: http://aei.pitt.edu/1007/, retrieved on March 4, 2020.

Desai, Mihir A. and Dharmapala, Dhammika, *Corporate tax avoidance and high powered incentives, economics working papers department of economics*, Mansfield, University of Connecticut, UCONN Library, 2004.

Douma, Sjoerd, *Optimization of tax sovereignty and free movement*, IBFD Doctoral Series, No. 21, Amsterdam, IBFD Publications BV, October 6, 2011, available at: https://ssrn.com/abstract=2997412

European Commission, *Guide to the case law of the European court of justice on articles 56 et seq. TFEU – Freedom to provide services*, available at: http://ec.europa.eu/docsroom/translations/renditions/pdf

Evertsson, Nubia, State aid and taxation of transnational companies: a study of state-corporate crime, *Crit Crim*, 25, 507–522, 2017, doi: 10.1007/s10612-017-9375-6

Faulhaber, Lilian V., Sovereignty, integration and tax avoidance in the European Union: striking the proper balance, *Columbia Journal of Transnational Law*, 48, 177, 2009–2010, available at: https://scholarship.law.georgetown.edu/facpub/1838

Furman, Jason, *The concept of neutrality in tax policy*, available at: www.brookings.edu/wp-content/uploads/2016/06/0415_tax-_neutrality_furman-1.pdf

Ghosh, J., Tax law and the internal market: a critique of the principle of mutual recognition, *Cambridge Yearbook of European Legal Studies*, 16, 189–221, 2014, doi: 10.1017/S1528887000002597

Gordon, Jeff, Coherent capital structure policy: between bailouts and the interest deduction, *Yale Law School*, 1182–1211, 2021, available at: https://openyls.law.yale.edu/bitstream/handle/20.500.13051/8342/09._Gordon_Note._Final._1182_1225.pdf?sequence=2&isAllowed=y, retrieved on January 15, 2022.

Gravelle, Jane G., *Tax havens: international tax avoidance and evasion*, Ithaca, Cornell University ILR School DigitalCommons@ILR, 2015.

Hagen, J.V. and Hammond, G.W., Regional insurance against asymmetric shocks: an empirical study for the European Community, *The Manchester School*, 66, 331–353, 1998, doi: 10.1111/1467-9957.00104

Hale, Geoffrey, Navigating disruption: the politics of business tax reform as two-level game, *Canadian Tax Journal/Revue fiscale canadienne*, 67(3), 667–692, 2019, doi:10.32721/ctj.2019.67.3.sym.hale

Head, John W. (John Warren), *Global business law: principles and practice of international commerce and investment*, 3rd ed., Durham, NC, Carolina Academic Press, 2012.

Hegland, Kenney F., *Introduction to the study and practice of law in a nutshell*, 6th ed., St. Paul, MN, West Academic Publishing, 2014.

Heller, M., Globalization, the new economy, and the commodification of language and identity, *Journal of Sociolinguistics*, 7, 473–492, 2003.

Herb, Michael, No representation without taxation? Rents, development, and democracy, *Comparative Politics*, 37(3), 297–316, April 2005, published by: Ph.D. Program in Political Science of the City University of New York Stable, available at: www.jstor.org/stable/20072891

Herdegen, Matthias, *Principles of international economic law*, 1st ed., Oxford, Oxford University Press, 2013.

Jaakkola, Jussi, A democratic dilemma of european power to tax: reconstructing the symbiosis between taxation and democracy beyond the state?, *German Law Journal; Toronto*, 20(5), 660–678, July 2019, doi: 10.1017/glj.2019.55

Jackson, John H. (John Howard), *International economic relations: cases, materials, and text on the national and international regulation of transnational economic relations*, St. Paul, MN, New York University School of Law, West, 2013.

Jaeger, Thomas, Tax concessions for multinationals: in or out of the reach of state aid law?, *Journal of European Competition Law & Practice*, 8(4), 2017.

Kane, Mitchell, Considering "reconsidering the taxation of foreign income", *Tax Law Review*, 62, 2009, available at: https://ssrn.com/abstract=2145394

Keightley, Mark P. and Stupak, Jeffrey M., *Corporate tax base erosion and profit shifting (BEPS): an examination of the data, congressional research data*, 2015, https://digital.library.unt.edu/ark:/67531/metadc816234/

Khan Niazi, Shafi U. and Krever, Richard, Romance and divorce between international law and EU law: implications for European competence od direct taxes, *Stanford Journal of International Law, no. 53*:2 2017, ISSN: 0731–5082, Author/Editor: Stanford University, Publisher: Stanford University – School of Law.

Kirsch, Clifford E., *Financial product fundamentals: law, business, compliance*, 2nd ed., New York, Practising Law Institute, 2012.

Klare, Karl E., Judicial deradicalization of the Wagner act and the origins of modern legal consciousness, 1937–1941, *Minnesota Law Review*, 1732, 1978, available at: https://scholarship.law.umn.edu/mlr/1732, retrieved on March 20, 2020.

Kuzniacki, Błażej, *Tax avoidance through controlled foreign companies under European Union law with specific reference to poland, accounting, economics, and law: a convivium*, Berlin, de Gruyter, 2017.

Lang, Michael, Pistone, Pasquale, Schuch, Josef, Staringer, Claus and Storck, Alfred, *Corporate income taxation in Europe: the common consolidated corporate tax base (CCCTB) and third countries*, Cheltenham, Edward Elgar Publishing Limited, 2013, E-ISBN 978 1 78254 542 2.

Leijon, Karin, National courts and preliminary references: supporting legal integration, protecting national autonomy or balancing conflicting demands?, *West European Politics*, 2020, doi: 10.1080/01402382.2020.1738113

Lenaerts, Koen and Gutman, Kathleen, "Federal common law" in the European Union: a comparative perspective from the United States, *American Journal of Comparative Law*, 54, 1–121, 2006, doi:10.1093/ajcl/54.1.1

Lewis, Meredith, *Kolsky, Frankel, Susy, International economic law and national autonomy*, New York, Cambridge University Press, 2010.

Lianos, Ioannis and Sokol, D. *Daniel, The global limits of competition law*, Stanford, CA, Stanford Law Books, 2012.

López Espadafor, Carlos María, Lagunas en el Derecho Tributario de la Unión Europea – Gaps in the tax law of the European Union, *Cuadernos de Derecho Transnacional*, 9(2), 375–407, Octubre 2017, ISSN 1989–4570, available at: www.uc3m.es/cdt; doi: 10.20318/cdt.2017.3878

López Espadafor, Carlos María, Tax justice issues in the European Union = Cuestiones de justicia tributaria en la Unión Europea, *Cuadernos de Derecho Transnacional*, 11(2), 230–252, Octobre 2019, ISSN 1989–4570, available at: www.uc3m.es/cdt; doi: 10.20318/cdt.2019.4956

Lotito Fedele, S., The Ne Bis In idem principle in tax law: European and Italian frameworks, *Central European Public Administration Review*, 18(1), 51–68, 2020, available at: https://orcid.org/0000-0003-0108-9863

Loughrey, Joan, *Corporate lawyers and corporate governance*, Cambridge, New York, Cambridge University Press, 2011.

Malawer, Stuart S., *Global trade and international law*, Buffalo, NY, William S. Hein & Co., Inc., 2012.

Marchgraber, Christoph, The avoidance of double non-taxation in double tax treaty law: a critical analysis of the subject-to-tax clause recommended by the European commission, *EC Tax Review*, 23(5), 293–302, 2014, available at: https://kluwerlawonline.com/journalarticle/EC+Tax+Review/23.5/ECTA2014027, retrieved on January 15, 2022.

Marise, Cremona, Peter, Hilpold, Nikos Schneider, Lavranos and Staiger, Stefan, *R. Ziegler, Andreas, reflections on the constitutionalisation of international economic law: liber amicorum for Ernst-Ulrich Petersmann*, Leiden, Martinus Nijhoff Publishers, 2014.

Markham, Jerry W., *Corporate finance: debt, equity, and derivative markets and their intermediaries*, 3rd ed., St. Paul, MN, Thomson/West, 2011.

Masouros, Pavlos E., *Corporate law and economic stagnation: how shareholder value and short-termism contribute to the decline of the Western economies*, The Hague, The Netherlands, Eleven International Publishing, 2013.

Maynard, Therese H., *Business planning: financing the start-up business and venture capital financing*, New York, Wolters Kluwer Law & Business, Aspen Publishers, 2010.

McGee, Robert W., *The ethics of tax evasion – perspectives in theory and practice*, New York, Springer Science and Business Media, LLC, 2012, doi:10.1007/978-1-4614-1287-8

McGowan, Michael, Thomson, Andrew and Hardwick, Emma, Preventing treaty abuse, *Tax Journal Insight and Analysis*, 2015, available at: www.taxjournal.com

Mendoza, Enrique G., Quadrini, Vincenzo and Rıos-Rull, Jose-Vıctor, Financial integration, financial deepness and global imbalances, *Journal of Political Economy*, 117(3), 2009, available at: www.journals.uchicago.edu/doi/pdfplus/10.1086/599706?casa_token=v7rgCxMSa9MAAAAA%3AR2Zka5IV5jQjhONhL_VT49ZpiBfJoLB4x5L5-YMLGipLwBzwTUNyN7KuToSte-UmRHYX3ySuwfs&, retrieved on May 20, 2020.

Mihaela, Tofan, *Tax law*, Bucharest, CH Beck Publishing House, 2016.

Moore, Marc T., *Corporate governance in the shadow of the state*, Portland, OR, Hart, 2013.

Morgan, J.A., Taxing the powerful, the rise of populism and the crisis in Europe: the case for the EU common consolidated corporate tax base, *International Politics*, 1–19, 2017, ISSN 1384–5748, doi: 10.1057/s41311-017-0052-x

Mullerat, Ramon, *Corporate social responsibility: the corporate governance of the 21st century*, 2nd ed., New York, Wolters Kluwer Law & Business, 2011.

Nogueira, Pinto, Félix, João, Pistone, Pasquale, Lazarov, Ivan and Turina, Alessandro, Abuse through the use of shell companies and arrangements for tax purposes in the European Union: feedback on the EU consultation by the IBFD task force on EU law, *International Tax Studies*, 7, July 14, 2021, Journal Articles & Opinion Pieces IBFD, available at: https://ssrn.com/abstract=, retrieved on December 20, 2021.

Novoa, Cesar Garcia, Tax neutrality in the exercise of the right of establishment within the EU and the funding of companies, *Intertax*, 38, 2010.

OECD, *Action plan on base erosion and profit shifting*, Paris, OECD Publishing, 2013, doi:10.1787/9789264202719-en

OECD, *Statement by the OECD/G20 inclusive framework on BEPS on the two-pillar approach to address the tax challenges arising from the digitalisation of the economy*, OECD/G20 Inclusive Framework on BEPS, Paris, OECD, January 2020, avaiable at: www.oecd.org/tax/beps/statement-by-the-oecd-g20-inclusive-framework-on-beps-january-2020.pdf

OECD, *Tax challenges arising from digitalisation – interim report 2018: inclusive framework on BEPS, OECD/G20 base erosion and profit shifting project*, Paris, OECD Publishing, 2018, doi:10.1787/9789264293083-en

Orbach, Barak, *Regulation: why and how the state regulates*, New York, NY, Foundation Press, 2013.

Pacces, Alessio M., *Rethinking corporate governance: the law and economics of control powers*, Abingdon, Oxon, New York, Routledge, 2012.

Pantazatou, Katerina, Economic and political considerations of the court's case law post crisis: an exemple from tax law and the internal market, *CYELP*, 9, 77–118, 2013.

Pato, Antonio Calisto, Cross-border direct tax issues of investment funds from the perspective of European law, *EC Tax Review*, 5, 2008.

Perez, Jose Domingo Palomino, *Are the LOB provisions efficient measures to prevent tax treaty hopping by taxpayers?*, Tilburg, Tilburg University, 2017.

Pinto, Arthur R., *Understanding corporate law*, 4th ed., New Providence, NJ, LexisNexis, 2013.

Pistone, Pasquale, Towards European international tax law, *EC Tax Review*, 1, 2005.

Ponomareva, Karina, Principles of subsidiarity and proportionality in European tax law, *Financial Law Review*, 10(2), 2018.

Posner, Richard A., *Economic analysis of law*, 8th ed., New York, Aspen Publishers, 2011.

Povazanova, Kristina and Kovaciková, Hana, Multinational tax avoidance vs. European Commission, *Bratislava Law Review*, 1, 2017.

Pun, Gregory, Base erosion and profit shifting: how corporations use transfer pricing to avoid taxation, *Boston College International and Comparative Law Review*, 40(2), 2017.

Ramirez, Steven A., *Lawless capitalism: the subprime crisis and the case for an economic rule of law*, New York, New York University Press, 2013.

Report of the fiscal and financial committee (neumark report), 1962, available at: http://aei.pitt.edu/34508/1/A677.pdf, retrieved on March 3, 2020.

Report to the council and the commission on the realization by stages of the economic and monetary union in the community – Werne report, 1970, available at: https://aei.pitt.edu/1002/1/monetary_werner_final.pdf, retrieved on March 2, 2020.

Reuven, Avi-Yonah, International tax evasion: what can be done?, *American Prospect Lonform*, 2016.

Reuven, Avi-Yonah, The three goals of taxation, *Tax Law Review*, 60(1), 1–28, 2006.

Ribstein, Larry E., *The rise of the uncorporation*, New York, Oxford University Press, 2010.

Richard, Kyle, Are all tax rulings state aid? Examining the European Commission recent state aid decisions, *Houston Business and Tax Law Journal*, XVIII, ISSN: 1543–2602.

Richards, Eric L., *Legal and ethical aspects of international business*, New York, Wolters Kluwer Law & Business, 2014.

Robert, Schütze, Two-and-a-half ways of thinking about the European Union, *Politique européenne*, 3(53), 28–37, 2016, available at: www.cairn.info/revue-politique-europeenne-2016-3-page-28.htm

Rosenbloom, H. David, International tax policy: a view from the US, *Australian Law Review*, 41(3), 2012.

Ruding, Onno, *Report of the committee of independent experts on company taxation*, Executive summary, March 1992, EU Commission – Working Document, available at: http://aei.pitt.edu/8702/, retrieved on March 5, 2020.

Schreiber, Ulrich and Fuhrich, Gregor, European group taxation-the role of exit taxes, *European Journal of Law and Economics*, 27, 257–274, 2009, doi: 10.1007/s10657-008-9090-6, Published online December 24, 2008, Springer Science and Business Media, LLC.

Schreiber, Ulrich, *International company taxation: an introduction to the legal and economic principles*, Berlin, Heidelberg, Springer-Verlag, 2013, ISBN 978-3-642-36305-4, doi: 10.1007/978-3-642-36306-1

Schultz, Thomas (Lawyer), *Transnational legality: stateless law and international arbitration*, 1st ed., Oxford, Oxford University Press, 2014.

Schwarz, Stephen, *Fundamentals of corporate taxation: cases and materials*, 8th ed., New York, Foundation Press, Thomson Reuters, 2012.

Segre, Claudio. *The development of a European capital market*, Report of a Group of Experts appointed by the EEC Commission, 1966, available at: http://aei.pitt.edu/31823/, retrieved on March 1, 2020.

Shackelford, Scott J., *Managing cyber attacks in international law, business, and relations: in search of cyber peace*, New York, Cambridge University Press, 2014.

Shaviro, Daniel, *Fixing U.S. international taxation*, Oxford, Oxford University Press, 2014.

Slemrod, J. and Gillitzer, C., Insights from a tax-systems perspective, *CESifo Economic Studies*, 60, 1–31, November 2013, doi: 10.1093/cesifo/ift015

Stephan, Paul B., *International business and economics: law and policy*, 4th ed., New Providence, NJ, LexisNexis, 2010.

Sting, Anna, Company tax integration in the European Union during economic crisis – why and how?, *Erasmus Law Review*, 1, 2014, available at: www.eraslawreview.nl/; https://heinonline.org

Summers, Robert S., *Contract and related obligation: theory, doctrine, and practice*, 6th ed., St. Paul, MN, West, 2011.

Tang, Zheng Sophia, *Jurisdiction and arbitration agreements in international commercial law*, Milton Park, Abingdon, Oxon and New York, Routledge, 2014.

Tenore, Mario, The transfer of assets from a permanent establishment to its general enterprise in the light of European tax law, *International Tax Review Intertax*, 34(8–9), 2006.

Terra, Ben J.M. and Peter, Wattel, *European tax law hardcover*, Alphen aan den Rijn, Wolters Kluwer, Law & Business, 2008.

Tofan, Mihaela, Argument for ruling a unique European tax, *Journal of Modern Accounting and Auditing*, 7(10), 2011.

Tofan, Mihaela, *European financial law*, Iaşi, Romania, University Alexandru Ioan Cuza of Iasi Publishing House, 2019, ISBN 978-606-714-544-1

Tofan, Mihaela, *State right to rule tax system vis-à-vis multilateral regulation on new nexus and income allocation*, Cluj Tax Forum No. 7, 2019, available at: https://heinonline.org/HOL/LandingPage?handle=hein.journals/cluj2019&div=50&id=&page=, retrieved on October 15, 2021.

Tofan, Mihaela, The challenges of the CCTB/CCCTB project: from harmonisation to tax integration in the European Union, *Cluj Tax Forum Journal*, 15, 2019, available at: https://heinonline.org/HOL/LandingPage?handle=hein.journals/cluj2019&div=17&id=&page=

Van den Noord, P., *tax incentives and house price volatility in the euro area: theory and evidence*, OECD Economics Department Working Papers, No. 356, Paris, OECD Publishing, 2003, doi:10.1787/410243688730

Van Thiel, Servaas, The direct income tax case law of the European court of justice: past, trends and future developments, *Tax Law Review*, 62, 2008, ISSN: 0040–0041, Author/Editor: New York University School of Law, Publisher: Warren, Gorham & Lamont Series: Current periodical series, Language: English, Country of publication: United States of America.

Vanistendael, Frans, Halifax and Cadbury Schweppes: one single European theory of abuse in tax law?, *EC Tax Review*, 4, 2006.

Varallo, Gregory V., *Fundamentals of corporate governance: a guide for directors and corporate counsel*, 2nd ed., Chicago, IL, American Bar Association, Business Law Section, 2009.

Wang, Faye Fangfei, *Law of electronic commercial transactions: contemporary issues in the EU, US and China*, 2nd ed., London, Routledge, 2014.

Weber, Denis, The reasonableness test of the principal purpose test rule in OECD BEPS action 6 (tax treaty abuse) versus the EU principle of legal certainty and the EU abuse of law case law, *Erasmus Law Review*, 1, 2017.

Weiler, J.H.H., Federalism and constitutionalism, Europe's Sonderweg, in *The federal vision: legitimacy and levels of governance in the United States and the European Union*, Oxford, Oxford University Press, 2001.

Williamson, Vanessa, *Paying taxes: understanding Americans' tax attitudes*, Doctoral dissertation, Harvard University, Graduate School of Arts & Sciences, Cambridge, 2015.

Wolfgang, Schon, *Abuse of rights and European tax law*, available at: www.cambridge.org/core, retrieved on July 23, 2020.

Index

For Product Safety Concerns and Information please contact our EU representative GPSR@taylorandfrancis.com Taylor & Francis Verlag GmbH, Kaufingerstraße 24, 80331 München, Germany

Printed and bound by CPI Group (UK) Ltd, Croydon, CR0 4YY

14/09/2026

02216243-0010